MY

EXTRAORDINARY EXPERIENCES

QUESTIONING THE ESSENCE OF LIFE

VIVIANA VERHEESEN

BALBOA.
PRESS

A DIVISION OF HAY HOUSE

Balboa Press books may be ordered through booksellers or by contacting:

Balboa Press
A Division of Hay House
1663 Liberty Drive
Bloomington, IN 47403
www.balboapress.com.au
1 (877) 407-4847

Because of the dynamic nature of the Internet, any web addresses or
links contained in this book may have changed since publication and
may no longer be valid. The views expressed in this work are solely those
of the author and do not necessarily reflect the views of the publisher,
and the publisher hereby disclaims any responsibility for them.

The author of this book does not dispense medical advice or prescribe the use
of any technique as a form of treatment for physical, emotional, or medical
problems without the advice of a physician, either directly or indirectly. The
intent of the author is only to offer information of a general nature to help
you in your quest for emotional and spiritual well-being. In the event you use
any of the information in this book for yourself, which is your constitutional
right, the author and the publisher assume no responsibility for your actions.

The real names of the people mentioned throughout this book
have been changed in order to respect their privacy.

Any people depicted in stock imagery provided by Thinkstock are models,
and such images are being used for illustrative purposes only.
Certain stock imagery © Thinkstock.

Print information available on the last page.

ISBN: 978-1-5043-0424-5 (sc)
ISBN: 978-1-5043-0425-2 (e)

Balboa Press rev. date: 10/11/2016

ABOUT THE AUTHOR

A T SEVEN, VIVIANA VERHEESEN sailed with her parents onboard a migrant ship from Holland to Australia. Having experienced many events outside of normal everyday life, Viviana has always known that these would eventually lead her to write this book.

Viviana has travelled extensively and resides in tropical North Queensland Australia.

You may reach Viviana Verheesen at www.vivianaverheesen.com

INTRODUCTION

M Y NAME IS VIVIANA. I'm an ordinary person who has experienced extraordinary things. I am neither psychic, nor scientist. I'm not a spiritual master, nor am I trained in any such matters. I follow no religion and belong to no label. I believe that there is only one truth and that we are all a part of that truth.

The incredible experiences described in this book started at eight years of age and continued throughout my life. No one around me seemed to be experiencing anything like the events that I was experiencing. Like anything amazing that happens in one's life, it is human nature to want to share it with others. Because these events didn't fit into normal everyday life, I quickly learnt that these were best left unspoken and to my greatest frustration, I have had to heavily suppress myself from sharing them for much of my life.

It is both a great relief and release that at 62 years, I am finally able to share these events openly.

This book is a record of many of the unusual events that have challenged everything that I have been taught about life. It is also a log of my progressive thought process as I try to logically piece together each event and how it could possibly fit into what we perceive our life to be.

Not all of my events have been recorded.

I believe that everyone has experienced such events to some degree, but we easily dismiss what we can't comprehend, or merely go into denial and choose to forget what is too difficult to understand. It is an incredibly difficult task to break through the barriers of a life of conditioning.

Anyone who hasn't had such experiences may find these events hard to believe. Nevertheless these are my experiences, and this is my *truth*. I implore you, the reader, to keep an open mind, as I believe that only an open mind can discover the "more" in one's life and that a closed mind cannot open the door to what is available.

My reasons for writing this book are many:

Above all, I feel *obligated* to write it.

I have written for people who sense that there is more to this life and who are searching for information. It is also to comfort and encourage those who have had similar experiences but are too afraid to speak out for fear of ridicule.

And I have written in the hope that religious and spiritual communities may find commonality in their beliefs and come to understand that regardless of religious labels, we are all of the same.

It is my personal gift to you, the reader. I hope that this book will inspire a sense of inquisitiveness into your own existence and assist you in understanding that you are a unique part of a greater whole throughout your journey in this brief moment called life.

—Viviana Verheesen

I would like to give gratitude to all the people who have
in some way assisted me in bringing this book to fruition.
I would also like to give gratitude to the
people throughout my life
who have always been there to listen
and allowed me to share openly
and without judgement.
no words can ever thank you enough.

To those people who have had similar experiences
with little chance to comfortably share,
take comfort in knowing
that you are not alone.

CONTENTS

EVENT 1

The Mystery Begins

A s NEW MIGRANTS, WE had been invited to accompany Mrs B, who had lived in Australia for some years, on a long journey through the Australian countryside. I was around eight and a half years of age at the time.

After many hours on the road, my younger brother needed the toilet, so my mother asked Mrs B where the next toilet was. At that moment, I became filled with incredible excitement because all of a sudden, without ever having been there, I knew *exactly* where the toilet was and how to get there.

Can you imagine what that was like for an eight-year-old?

With electrifying excitement and almost jumping out of my seat, I squealed out to my mother at the top of my voice, "Mum! Mum! I know where the toilet is! I know where the toilet is!"

I didn't know *how* I knew, but I *knew* that I knew, and I *knew* that I was *right*.

My mother turned to face me with a frustrated look. "Stop yelling!"

She turned to listen to Mrs B, who replied, "We will soon be in the next town. There's a public toilet there."

I was so excited that I was unable to contain myself and excitedly continued yelling, "Mum! Mum! I know! I know! I know! Mum, I know!" My words were flying out like rockets. "Mum, we turn left at the road with the grass in the middle! Mum! Mum! We go to the top of the hill and go left! And Mum, there's a milk bar on the left with a red door! And Mum, the toilet is in the middle of the road in front of the milk bar! Mum! Mum!"

My mother wasn't taking any notice of what I was saying and yelled at me again to keep quiet.

I was totally frustrated. I was having an amazing experience seeing into the future, and nobody was listening.

"But Mum! The counter is on the right when you go in! Mum, I know! I know! I know where it is!"

At the realization that no matter how hard I yelled, everyone was just continuing to do their own thing and not taking any notice, I fell back into my seat and withdrew into a silent world of my own, feeling somewhat deserted.

I will never forget how I felt as I sat quietly in the back seat of the car when we drove into that town.

In a quiet, stunned state of shock, I took in the scenery, confirming everything that I had already seen in my mind.

It was exactly as I had seen it. We drove into town until we came to a road with a grass median down the middle. We turned left and drove up the hill. At the top of the hill, we turned left again, as I *knew* we would. There was a milk bar on the left with a red door, and the toilet was opposite the milk bar in the middle of the road.

Still in my silent world, I was now trying to figure out how I could have possibly seen all this when I had never been there before. A million questions rushed through my young, inexperienced mind.

After my mother and brother came out of the toilet block, I followed them into the milk bar. It too was just as I had seen it in my mind.

How was that possible?

How incredibly isolated and alone I felt at that time.

If only people had stopped and listened to me. But they hadn't, and now here was the proof that I had seen into a future place, and no one was there to share or witness this with me. The internal questioning that followed totally absorbed me to the point where I don't remember what happened for the rest of the day – or what the rest of the holiday was about. I had entered my isolated world, and a mystery beyond my understanding had changed me. There was more going on than what I had so far been told about life. The mystery had begun, and so had my search for answers.

I pondered on this event in my life as a child for many years and knew that I would not rest until I understood what had happened.

Five years later, I started to figure things out.

Approaching thirteen years of age in the 1960s, I'd been given a transistor radio and was sitting on the small brick wall in front of our house with my "tranny" to my ear. The mystery of seeing into the future five years earlier was still haunting my mind, and I was desperate to understand it logically, but nobody had yet been able to give me anything that resembled a logical answer – let alone take me seriously.

As I was listening to the radio, I started contemplating, *How can I be hearing people talk on this radio without an electrical cord plugged in? How can voices be invisibly carried through the air from a faraway place to this box thing that somehow picks it up and then translates it to my ear so that I can hear what they are talking about in a place beyond my normal hearing reach?*

Suddenly, at the onset of my teenage years, the obvious answer had arrived.

It dawned on me that humans are capable of being transmitters and receivers just like radios and TVs. I realised that Mrs B had been there before and was remembering where the toilet was in her own mind, and I was able to receive the pictures in the same way that a television set picks up a picture transmitted by invisible wavelengths from elsewhere. How else could that occur?

I could logically conclude that humans must have the capacity and the capability of developing telepathy through somehow intercepting invisible wavelengths.

I finally had a logical answer that made sense.

Many similar events occurred throughout my life. Some of these will be referred to later in this book.

EVENT 2

An Invisible Playmate

NOT LONG AFTER I had concluded that we are capable of being transmitters and receivers, I was thrown another very different experience that couldn't be explained and is very difficult to put into a language designed only for our expression of a material world.

The words that I have chosen in my endeavour to share the experience with you, are the closest possible descriptions I can find. They are indeed not able to fully communicate the experience, as there are just no words to adequately describe it. I can only inform you that the experience was far more intense and exhilarating than any of these words can convey.

Every year from the age of eight until the age of fifteen, my mother, father, two siblings, and I, along with other families from our community, would take on the long, challenging dirt road with trailers and caravans in tow to Wilsons Promontory National Park. There, we set up camp for the six-week Christmas school holiday period.

The scenery was spectacular as the road meandered through mountains laced with giant orange granite boulders that disappeared into the deep sapphire-blue sea below.

How I just loved those massive boulders!

After everyone set up camp and had dinner, the dads would return home to continue working to support their families, returning only at weekends with supplies.

These were the most magical times of my life, although I have to say that I feel quite blessed with having had many magical times.

My mum would burst into new life during these holidays, always playing highly inventive practical jokes. She was totally in her element and was loads of fun to be around. She was a wonderful storyteller and a great poet who was always exciting to listen to. The child within my mother glistened during our time at "the prom."

The contrast between life at home in daily routine and these holidays taught me a lot about people and life itself. One of the greatest and most obvious lessons was just how beautifully people shine, given the right conditions. Another great lesson was how routine seemed to rob us of so much of our creativity. It seemed that everyone just blossomed during these holidays.

I enjoyed it all: the families, the friends, the place itself, and the fun times that we all shared. As children we were given almost limitless freedom while the mums enjoyed their own time as women together.

We would often go bush and explore the many walking tracks throughout the national park, but most of our days were spent down at the beach lazing beside an isolated bunch of large orange granite boulders. Our favourite was a massive flat rock that rose gently from beneath the sand and was surrounded by bigger boulders offering shelter when the breeze picked up.

For all those years that we holidayed in this magnificent place, this group of rocks was our ever-faithful meeting place. Life on that rock with family and friends was loads of fun and holds some of my dearest memories, but there were times when I just needed to go off and explore on my own to spend time by myself with my own thoughts. On these occasions, I would sneak off to the end of the beach, where a rim of huge granite boulders – some the size of houses – stretched out from the bottom of the mountain, reaching down and disappearing into the waters below.

For hours I would investigate these boulders and meander through the many caverns hidden amongst them, watching and listening to the powerful waves washing over them. I would peek into the many rock pools to see what little creatures I might find. There were sea anemones with red tentacles and I took great joy in sticking my fingers gently into these jelly-like creatures to feel them sucking on to me. Another great delight were the little 'squirties'; sea sponges exposed at low tide, which when you gently pushed down on them would squirt a jet of water up to a meter into the air!

Nearly every day, in this magical place, I would lose myself to time and felt such an affinity that the more familiar I became, the more *home* it became and like a spirited racehorse I would challenge myself, knowing exactly where to place my feet, to see how fast I could sprint over the rocks from one end to another.

It was here in this much loved place that I was to be thrown my next challenge in the mystery of life.

It was a most glorious, calm, sunny day. I had just started to run over the rocks for my playful speed challenge.

With my shiny long straight hair swishing around me, I ran and jumped from one rock to another, carrying with me a lovely feeling of freedom as I happily enjoyed each wonderful leap. Then all of a sudden something untoward happened:

Whoosh

"Oh my God! What's happening!?"

The world was no longer *normal* and the question of life confronted me yet again. I was no longer *in charge* of my own physical body and something *other than myself* had taken hold of me, lifting me up and carrying me at a speed faster than I could have possibly accomplished all on my own.

This was totally *unnatural* according to everything that I had ever experienced. *Something else was carrying my body* and I felt no weight. It certainly didn't fit in with my understanding of gravity. *Gravity* didn't even seem to be playing any part in what was occurring.

I was hardly touching the surface of the rocks, and as I continued to run, at times I felt that I had completely missed touchdown. I felt as light as a feather. I was desperately trying to understand in my mind what was occurring. It was both very strange and very exhilarating.

In the first instance I was totally shocked. This *whoosh* initially entered and carried me with quite a bit of force and I was completely taken by surprise. I was confused, a little afraid, and in wonderment all at the same time. Shortly after the initial shock, I began to feel an incredible and immense joy and the fear completely subsided.

So there I was, running like the wind without any effort on my part and not even having to think about where to place my feet, because *I certainly wasn't the one doing the running*. Something else was doing the running and whatever was *running me* felt *inconceivably amazing*. There are simply no words in the English language to describe the feeling of this experience. It was an immeasurably beautiful and very endearing feeling.

Can you imagine this happening to you? Something other than yourself takes your body for a run? How does one describe that?

The feelings experienced as *we* ran like the wind itself with amazing leaps and bounds over the rocks simply put, can't be adequately explained but I will endeavour to continue to share it with you.

I experienced a joy beyond any joy that I had ever felt before. My fear had completely dissolved. I felt totally safe and was able to completely surrender to allow whatever was happening to me, to happen (as if I knew how to stop this anyway).

The more relaxed I became, the more I could feel what was happening. I continued to feel as light as a feather without any sense of weight at all, which was immensely liberating.

Then I had the most amazing moment of *understanding* which I can only express as being *cleared* to me (I really don't know how to describe this), and then I *knew*.

And trust me, this is going to sound incredibly *bizarre*.

My body had been joined by an aboriginal boy's spirit who was of my age group and who had also, like me, taken great joy in running over these magnificent rocks in his own physical life.

This was his country, and this was his final resting place.

His personality had joined me in my body in order to once again experience the great physical delight of running over these magnificent boulders, as he had done many times in his own life.

(It takes great courage to be writing this down in a world where such events are both rare and not easily accepted.)

For most people this event is going to be very difficult to believe, and I know that I am really *putting myself out there* by sharing this with you.

Nevertheless, regardless of just how bizarre this event sounds or what people will think of me, it is time to share what I have experienced and what has been waiting for almost a lifetime to be shared.

It was indeed one of the most magical, blissful, and endearing events of my life. We had "united" into inseparable playmates "in love" (not of the romantic type), playing *together* as one under the sun.

Throughout the event, we were *both* ecstatically happy and in total unison, yet we were still aware of our separate identities. We were both immensely delighted in running over the rocks *together* at superhuman speed and sharing this delightful experience *with each other*. We were indeed *ultimate playmates*.

It was unbelievably, *lovingly electric.*

Two personalities joined in one spirit, or should I say two spirits in one body, doing what both delighted in doing, together, as one, inseparable.

Just when I thought that I had figured out that we are transmitters and receivers and I could finally get on with living a normal life without incessant questioning, I was now faced with a whole new experience to be sorted out.

A new list of questions bombarded my mind. How was this possible?

Let me share a phrase that I once read which has been of great benefit in my search for truth and I feel would be appropriate to share with you at this point;

"Only an open mind will ever be able to know the secrets of the universe."

I have never forgotten that phrase. I totally believe that to be true, and I toast and commend those who can keep an open mind when everything they have ever been taught about their life defies that such an experience is even possible.

I know that if I hadn't had this experience myself, I would find myself struggling to accept this. I can only reiterate again: this is as real an experience to me as the experience of you reading this is to you.

Barely a teenager, I had not yet had enough life experience to be able to answer the constant barrage of new questions invading my mind. I could only deduce at this stage from this experience that invisible personalities existed and that they were as much alive as I was.

I could also conclude that obviously our personality didn't fill up our whole body entirely because I had just experienced that at least two personalities could be in one body at the same time.

Questions remained to be answered:

"Where in the body does the personality reside?"

"How much volume of the physical body does the personality require?"

"How can two individual personalities unite as "one" in the same body and share the exact same experience and yet maintain their own separate awareness?"

This was way beyond anything that I had learnt at school and I knew no other person that I could even turn to for answers. Life had certainly presented me with some intriguing things to explore! This was not the only such incident that I was to experience and I will refer to that later in the book.

Fascinating!

EVENT 3

Saved by the Same Stranger, Twice

M Y INSATIABLE YEARNING TO explore the world took hold very early in my life.

It started when my mother would allow us to play in the street just outside the front of the house. She would instruct my older sibling and me to play within the closest two power poles and not to venture beyond them.

As soon as my mother was out of sight, I bolted beyond the poles, jumping, skipping, and running, wherever my little young legs would take me, to explore the streets of the Dutch fishing village where I was born.

Eventually and usually all too soon, my freedom would come to an end as either nature called or my thirst needed quenching.

That would be followed by a knock on the nearest door for assistance.

I was always delighted when doors opened because they were always opened by fully grown adults who had to adjust their initial greet from staring straight out, to looking down below their waist with a great look of surprise on their face.

Then came the same old questions; "Hallo, waar is jouw Mama?' or "Wat is jouw naam"? or "Waar woon jij??' which in English translates to "Hello, Where is your Mother?", "What is your name?" and "Where do you live?"

I would reply, "Ik moet plassen," which is Dutch for "I have to do wee," or 'Ik heb dorst," meaning "I am thirsty".

People always showered me with kindness and helped me with whichever was relevant.

Most doors were usually opened by women and I hold some dear memories of life at that time but I remember one day an old man opened the door when I was in desperate need to go to the toilet. He had a walking stick and, holding my hand, walked me ever so slowly to the toilet. I was scared that I might wet my pants. Luckily I was able to hold on, and he helped me onto the toilet. I remember how lovely and kind he was. Afterwards he grabbed my hand again and led me to a big table where he gave me the tallest glass of lemonade that I think till this day I have ever had to face.

As I was still too young to tell people where I lived, these door knocks eventually led me to the local police station, which became another home.

I loved those wonderful, friendly policemen. I got lots of yummy biscuits, and they always gave me a beautiful little train to play with. They had come to know me and where I lived, and eventually they would pop me on a bicycle and take me home. Such great memories!

I often think of how vulnerable I was at that young age and how lucky I was that nothing untoward ever happened to me.

When I was seven, my parents decided to move from our picture-perfect fishing village in Holland, which I totally loved, to an industrial town built for coal mining in Australia. I missed terribly the village where I was born, along with all of my rather large extended family and the friends that I had made on my wanderings. I felt such a long way from home, and to this day, I have always missed that village and the extended family life that I experienced as a child in Holland.

I was fifteen years of age when I grabbed the reins to my own life and left Victoria to work in Sydney for a year, after which I moved to Melbourne and worked for another year. By then, I had saved enough money for a one-way ticket to somewhere, anywhere, and I didn't care where. I just wanted to go wandering again to explore the world, and with the help of my parents, I was able to organize my own passport. Once I had my passport in my hand, the seconds were ticking.

I had managed to save up eight hundred dollars. I had no idea where I wanted to go. I just knew that I wanted to explore the world, and because I'd had such a fun time on our six-week cruise migrating from Holland to Australia, I wanted to go by boat.

On my first free day off from work, I decided to head into the city and spend the day checking out the travel agencies.

If a travel agency had posters in the window highlighting Brazil as a destination, I would go in and approach the travel agent with "Hi, I would like to travel to Brazil by boat. Do you have anything available, and if so, how much would it cost?"

The answer was usually a huge disappointment. It soon became clear that boat trips cost far more than flights because they would have to give you a room for two or more weeks and feed you at least three meals a day!

This was heartbreaking. I had spent the whole day going from agent to agent, collecting an armload of tantalizing travel brochures full of stunning photographs covering exotic places, and all beyond my financial reach.

It was nearing the end of the day, and businesses began preparing to close.

I had visited every travel agency that I had spotted, realizing that going by boat to wherever was going to cost at least two thousand dollars. It seemed that my measly eight hundred wasn't going to get me anywhere. At least not by boat.

Disillusioned, I headed off to catch the five-thirty bus home. The shops were already starting to close their doors, and there I was, now standing at the bus stop, hugging a giant armful of travel brochures, wondering how I was going to get my dream trip happening with only eight hundred dollars in the bank. It had taken two years to save that amount, and the thought that I might have to work and save up for another four years was too much to bear. I just had to go! There had to be a way! My feet were itching to go yesterday rather than tomorrow.

It had been a long day, and I was almost resigned to the fact that I wasn't going to go any time soon when all of a sudden my eyes fell upon a small travel agency just across the road from the bus stop. The sign on the door still showed "Open" and there were massive posters of Greece and Athens in the window. I couldn't believe my eyes. I had thought that I had been to them all, and that there were none left! How could I have missed that one? Immediately my adrenaline started pumping. All was not lost yet!

I checked for traffic, and there was my bus! I was hungry and tired, and I knew that if I didn't take this bus, I would have to wait an hour for the next one. I had to make a decision and be quick about it. *Do I catch the bus, or do I bolt into that travel agency before they turn the sign around to "Closed"?*

Before I could even work out what to do, I was asking the question, "Hi, I want to go to Greece by boat. Do you have anything available, and if so, how much would it cost?"

At that, the woman got up out of her seat, gave me a really sweet glance accompanied by a rather quirky smile as if she knew something that I didn't know, and said, to my surprise, "Hi, I'm Petra, take a seat." She then went to the door, turned the sign around, locked the door, and was now "Closed", and I was locked inside.

I hadn't ever been locked in by a business before, and it felt a little odd, yet at the same time I had a sense of anticipation that something was about to happen. I really didn't know what.

As she returned to her seat and sat down at her desk, I was captivated by her beauty, grace, and warmth and by the quirky smile still on her face. I felt a bit awkward in that I was holding her up from going home, and yet she seemed totally relaxed and dedicated to helping me regardless of how long it would take.

"Now, tell me, how can I help you?" she asked in an extremely relaxed manner.

She was so lovely and kind that I didn't want to waste her time, so I came out with the facts straight away.

"Well, you see, I really wish to travel somewhere by boat, and although I have been looking around all day, I have not been able to find a boat ticket for anything under two thousand dollars. I have been saving for two years, and I have already organized a passport, but I have only managed to save eight hundred dollars. I really want to go, and I don't want to travel by plane. Do you have any ideas as to how I can do this?"

Petra listened to me very attentively and I could see that she was genuinely interested in helping me. "Well, you are in luck. I have a one-way combination boat/plane fare to Greece, which departs Melbourne by boat for a two-week cruise to Singapore. After that, you are booked into a hotel at no cost to you where you will be on standby to fill the next empty plane seat to Greece, meaning you will need to be ready to travel at short notice to board your plane from Singapore to Athens."

She instantly captivated my attention; a mix of boat and plane might just be the answer! I continued to listen.

"It is cheaper for the organisers to put you up in a hotel for two weeks on standby rather than have an empty seat on either the boat or the plane. What this really means is that your journey from Melbourne to Greece is fully paid for with a free stopover in Singapore. If you can be flexible with your date of arrival in Greece, it is a very cheap way to travel. The great thing about this", she concluded, "is that the whole fare from Melbourne to Greece with the Singapore standby stopover at a five-star hotel will only cost you three hundred and thirty dollars."

Well! I nearly fell off my chair! Did she say three hundred and thirty dollars? Was I hearing right?

"Did you say three hundred and thirty dollars? All the way to Greece?" I asked.

"Yes. That's right. Three hundred and thirty dollars all the way to Greece," she responded, with that little strange quirky smile on her face.

Oh my God! I was electric with excitement. What a moment! It was the last Friday of April. Most of my friends were still in high school, and here I was booking a ticket overseas to explore the world. I was so excited … "I'll take it!"

And with that quirky smile on her face as if she had known all along that I was going to take this journey, Petra got up from the desk and walked to a filing cabinet to retrieve her bookings folder. Once seated, she opened the folder and began scanning for the next available travel date.

"We have a booking available in September," she said, lifting her eyes to look at my response.

I was not known for my patience, so my disappointment was enormous, to say the least. I quickly counted the months in my head. May, June, July, August, September, that was a whole five months away. Oh no, that would never do! I was so excited that I wanted to go yesterday!

"Wow, that's a long time away. Is there nothing earlier than that?"

"Afraid not, sorry. You see, because it is so cheap, it is always booked out well in advance," Petra responded.

I couldn't help but show my disappointment, as I was always one to display my feelings to the world in any instance. She gave me a most understanding and compassionate look.

There we were looking at each other in a moment of silence. She was so lovely, and I didn't know what to do. It was getting dark outside, and I felt a little bit lost.

Our silence was broken when the phone rang. She picked it up and answered, "Yes, Hello. Yes, you are lucky to have caught me, I am usually closed by now. How can I help?" she asked as she threw me a cheeky wink.

I sat in a daze. Lost to know what to do. I didn't want to go in September. I wanted to go soon.

After a short conversation over the phone, she thanked the caller, put the receiver down, and looked at me with that funny quirky smile again. "Well, aren't you a lucky one? That was a cancellation."

I was both excited and concerned. "Cancellation for when?" I asked.

"For this Thursday," she said, beaming her sparkling white teeth through her smile.

Oh my God! I counted the days, and that was in just six days' time!

It suddenly dawned on me that maybe I wasn't *that* ready! I had a job, was renting a house with three others, and had furniture, and a million other things went through my head all at once. I so wanted to go, but there was so much to do! Would I be able to do everything that I needed to do with only five days to prepare? This was truly a bittersweet moment! I so wanted this, but could I manage it?

Seeing my dilemma, Petra broke through my confusion: "I'll tell you what we can do. It is late, so I won't take any calls now until the morning. You can take the brochures home with you and have a think about it overnight. I will be opening the agency at eight thirty sharp tomorrow morning", she continued, "and the phone will start ringing as soon as I am in to see if there are any cancellations as it is very popular and this happens all the time. If you decide to take it, you must ring me first thing in the morning."

Phew! What a relief that was! I was so grateful for her suggestion. I had time to work out whether I could do everything I needed to do in just five days!

We said goodbye, and I headed to the bus stop. I knew that I had to get this sorted out because I had to go! My mind advanced full throttle into action: "I can give my furniture to my friends. I will have to visit my parents and leave some personal things with them. I'll have to give my work notice first thing in the morning. I'll need a list of what to take" – and so my mind raced all the way home!

After arriving home to "You're home late", I couldn't wait to share the day and everything that had happened with my wonderful friends.

I was the youngest of the household and I always looked up to the others. After I shared the events of my day, they could all see how badly I wanted to go, and on hearing of my dilemma with timing, they were all at the ready to pitch in and help make it happen. They were amazing, and I knew after speaking with them that I was going.

The next morning I started to ring the travel bureau before eight thirty, over and over. I was so worried that someone else would beat me that my finger was red from dialling.

"How can I help you?' Wow, I got through!

"I'll take it, I'll take it!'

"I thought you might", Petra said with a soft giggle in her tone. "I will book you in, but you will need to come in to see me as soon as possible today, as we have much to do. Bring in your passport. You will also need to do a tax return, so go to the post office and get a form; I will help you fill it in. You will also have to buy a backpack, and I recommend that you get the *H* frame. The sooner you come in, the better, as there is much for us to organise."

This was not your ordinary travel agent! Petra went beyond the extra mile. Maybe it was because I was still so young that she took me under her wing and arranged everything for me. She wrote a list of everything that I might need to take with me and even filled out and lodged my tax return.

I spent most of the afternoon racing in and out of her office. Petra would send me out to get some other form or something that I needed to buy for my trip and I would be off getting it. She was an absolute blessing. We filled in all the documents needed by various departments. She asked me all the questions, and what I didn't know, she just made up.

"Now there is only one thing more that we need to do and it is really very important," Petra explained. "You will need to have cholera and typhoid injections before entering Greece, so you will need to go to a medical clinic immediately, and be mindful to tell the doctor where you are going. Everything else is done. Don't worry about all the forms, as I will send them off for you tomorrow. Here is your ticket with all the details. Don't lose it as you will need it for boarding with your passport.

"Have a great time," she said as she gave me another one of her wonderful smiles. Petra was amazing, and I felt ever so grateful.

As for the cholera and typhoid injections; I hated getting injections but because Petra had told me that I needed to do that, I trusted her faithfully, and off to the doctor's I went.

"Ouch"! That really, really, hurt! Needles were still rather thick in those days.

"Now, these are only the first two injections. You will need to have another two injections in seven days," the doctor told me.

I felt instantly relieved. "Oh, but that won't be possible as I leave in five days' time," I said, hoping to get out of having them.

Alas, the doctor replied, "That's not a problem because I will give you the certificate to say that you have had both the cholera and typhoid injections, along with two injection ampoules and a letter for the ship's doctor. The doctor on board can complete the injections."

The doctor then wrote out a letter for the ship's doctor and with it also handed me a certificate to say that I had had the injections, along with the two ampoules.

"Now, do be very careful with these ampoules," he said as he handed them over.

The five days leading up to departure seemed like an eternity, and I thought that Thursday would never arrive. Finally the time came for me to embark on the Greek passenger boat, the *Patras*.

I took my place at the railing and looked down onto the pier where my friends and family were waving their goodbyes.

As I excitedly waved back, I remembered how we had waved goodbye to our extended families in Holland when we first embarked on the migrant ship bound for our new life in Australia. Now here I was, embarking on my own boat passage a decade later.

The ship blew its foghorn, and slowly we drifted away from the pier and off towards the horizon.

It was a magical moment and I was so very, very, young and incredibly naïve.

I could hardly believe it. I was on the boat. My dream had become a reality, and *no one* was going to make me get off, whether I gave the injections to the ship's doctor or not. I was on the boat.

I felt relieved as I naively threw those horrible two remaining ampoules overboard.

Life on board the *Patras* was everything that I had wished for and more. I was having the time of my life, dancing, sunning, swimming, making new friends, seeing amazing sunsets, and timelessly watching the wake at the back of the boat, staring out over the vast ocean in wonderment of it all.

Two weeks of sailing passed by all too quickly, and on arrival in Singapore I was transported to my five-star hotel. I was totally looked after during my five-day stay. I had come from a hard-working poor migrant family, and here I was, staying in a classy hotel surrounded by people that looked as if they had all just come out of a Hollywood movie. It was quite an experience, and it all felt a touch surreal. I was in awe of everything and I recall thinking that my backpack looked a trifle out of place.

I spent my time in Singapore either sightseeing or lazing in the sun by the pool, and on the fifth day I received a message that I was to catch a plane the following morning.

Everything had been organised smoothly, and we soon touched down in Greece.

I was a bit nervous handing over my passport to customs, as I was concerned that there might be repercussions from throwing my vaccinations overboard.

Wonderful! I got through customs, and my vaccination certificate wasn't even asked for! I could now relax and put that all behind me, or so I thought.

No one could speak English, and I couldn't speak Greek. There were five busses outside the airport, and I couldn't read any of the strange writing. I had no idea which bus to hop on and no one to communicate with.

This was in the time before the backpacking scene had established itself. A backpacker in this time was seen as a rare novelty, especially a female one.

I hopped on the first bus, and after what seemed a very long drive of a couple of hours, I began to wonder whether I was not heading to Athens at all but rather in the opposite direction. We were travelling on a small dirt road through sparse countryside when finally we passed what looked like a camping spot in the middle of nowhere. I took a mental note of it but stayed on the bus a while longer in the hope that we would soon get to Athens or somewhere other than empty arid land. As time went on, nothing changed, and I thought that my best shot would be to retrace my steps back to the airport and take a bus in the opposite direction from there.

With my backpack in hand, I headed to the front of the bus. "Can you stop the bus please? I want to get off," I said, pointing to the door.

The driver left me standing by the side of the road and watching the bus disappear into the distance, I wondered whether I had made the right decision. I turned back in the direction where I had come from and started a very long walk with my rather heavy, overloaded backpack filled with everything from books to high-heeled shoes and evening dresses, which only a true novice would pack.

I walked for hours before finally arriving at the deserted camping ground that I had spotted earlier.

Exhausted, I decided to stay to gather my strength and booked in for one night at the small kiosk before heading to a faraway tree behind a thick bush where I dropped my backpack and lay down on the ground to recuperate, hidden out of sight from the rest of the world and too exhausted to talk to anyone. Although there didn't seem to be anyone else around, I was tired and wanted to rest in solitude.

It didn't take long before I realized that something was very wrong. It was not like me *not* to have any energy, and yet I felt totally drained. I couldn't even manage to get my sleeping bag organised; all I could do was just lie there on the bare ground. I felt as if I had just been struck by something huge that I was unable to deal with, and I lay there like a dead weight for many hours until I drifted into an unconscious state.

The days that followed became a bit of a blur and quite scary. I woke up possibly the next morning or maybe even a few mornings later, still a dead weight and unable to move. I kept falling in and out of consciousness. I knew that I was in big trouble! I was very, very, ill indeed.

Being young and naïve, I didn't know that the first two injections the doctor had given me were to infect me with cholera and typhoid and that the second two injections, the ones I threw overboard, were the antidotes. If only the doctor had explained that to me. The huge and valuable lesson that this taught me, and one which, I have never forgotten to this day, is to *always* give an explanation regarding the reason behind any important request. I can't stress this enough. Failing to do so could cost someone *their life*.

So here I was, in a foreign country, suffering from both cholera and typhoid at the same time! My throat had swollen up terribly and I was unable to swallow. I was terrified that it was going to close up altogether and that I would not be able to get any air to breathe. My saliva was hot and plentiful, and being unable to swallow, it dribbled from my gaping mouth and ran down my cheek. My head had rolled into a small ditch and was lying lower than my body. I was completely depleted of any strength and unable to move or lift my head out of the ditch. All I could do was just lie there.

I was dying. I was in a faraway land, alone, in a place unlikely to be found in time for help, lying under a tree and hidden out of sight. The campground had been deserted, and the person who greeted me as I arrived probably thought that I had left early the next morning, and I was unable to call out.

I had to accept my fate. There was nothing that I could do.

I totally surrendered. I could still hear sounds in the distance, and occasionally I found the strength to briefly open my eyes and see the branches and sky above me. I could at least do that. I was incapable of anything else.

I don't know how long I had lain there drifting in and out of consciousness, with my mouth agape, still dribbling hot saliva, before I heard two very long, drawn-out, words:

"Hey, babe."

A male voice had spoken, and I opened my eyes to see a man standing over me. I was unable to reply. I couldn't speak or even make any movement of acknowledgement. All I could do was to just open my eyes for a moment and view him. Aware of the saliva still dribbling down my cheek, I knew I must have looked quite a sight. I was beyond caring and felt half dead by this stage.

As I stared at him, I wondered whether this man, this perfect stranger, was going to help me, or worse, had I gone beyond that point?

"You ain't lookin' too good, babe," he said in a strong American accent.

He obviously could see that I needed help and that I was totally at his mercy. All I knew about him was that he was dressed in a black Greek fisherman's cap, a black shirt, and jeans, and that he spoke English with an American accent and looked physically strong. I wanted to communicate but couldn't. All I could continue to do was to open my eyes for a brief moment and look vaguely in his direction before the lids fell closed again.

He knelt down and pushed one arm under my shoulders with his other arm under my knees and lifted me up with my head and arms dangling to the ground.

"My name is Tim from Seattle. You just hold on now, and we will get you some help." His kindness shone through and I knew that I was in good hands.

Tim carried me to the bus stop, and after quite a wait, a bus came along travelling in the opposite direction to the bus that I had taken from the airport.

We hopped on and ended up in Athens. I don't remember the journey.

I gained consciousness to see the ceiling of a long corridor as Tim carried me like a rag doll in his arms. I was still unable to speak or do anything and kept drifting in and out of consciousness.

I regained consciousness to find Tim, still holding me in his arms, speaking Greek with a female doctor in the corridor. I could make out her doctor's coat and stethoscope but was unable to look directly at her. I could see that this was going nowhere and that Tim was getting increasingly frustrated with her unwillingness to assist. After some arguing, and with obvious disappointment in her refusal to help, Tim carried me down the corridor again, and I faded out of consciousness, in complete surrender. I was beyond caring.

Again I regained consciousness, now slumped in a chair in a corner of a waiting area. I heard Tim speaking in Greek to another person in a white coat. With eyes barely open, I could make out shelves of boxed drugs from floor to ceiling. We were in some kind of pharmacy, and it was evident that the chemist had no interest in helping either. Tim was obviously determined not to leave without help and stood his ground for assistance. They engaged in heated discussion until finally the chemist handed over a bag full of medication.

Tim came over to me, laid me down on my back, placed the bag of drugs on my chest, lifted me up again like a ragdoll, and carried me, along with the big white bag of drugs, off to the bus as I lost consciousness.

I don't remember anything after that until one day I opened my eyes, and there was Tim, sitting next to me, leaning against my backpack under the tree.

I knew that I had come through it and I was going to survive. Tim had saved my life. What a remarkable stranger!

Tim greeted me with an enormous smile on his face. "We're getting there, babe. You'll be bouncing about in no time."

He lifted my head with his strong hand and gave me a drink. I was incredibly relieved to discover that I was finally able to swallow again.

I don't remember taking any medication or have any idea how Tim could have administered it while I was unconscious. Tim had stayed by my side and had nursed me back to the world of the living. He didn't speak about this time and was extremely humble about it.

We stayed in this camping ground for some weeks whilst Tim continued to look after me and feed me back to health. Once I had gathered my strength, Tim travelled with me for a month, ensuring that I was indeed OK before Tim departed to return to America. No words could ever describe how grateful I was for Tim's help.

These were the days before mobile phones and computers, and when we parted I felt sure that I would not see my friend Tim again. On that note we went our separate ways.

I travelled throughout southern Europe enjoying the different cultures and visiting many great places. I decided to go to Morocco despite all the warnings that young Western girls had gone missing there and that it would not be safe to travel alone in Morocco. With my naivety still fully intact, young, and with a mind of my own, I boarded a boat in the south of Spain and sailed off to Morocco.

Totally oblivious to the rules of how this society functioned, I got myself into some really tricky situations, which looking back is quite understandable. I was in a country where women were hardly seen at all, and if they were, they walked in silence five paces behind their husbands and young sons, fully clad from top to toe with only their face and ankles in view. And here I was, in my teens, wearing denim shorts, T-Shirt, and sandals, baring my head, neck, arms, and legs for everyone to see and doing exactly as I pleased. I was innocently having the time of my life without any awareness of the attention I was attracting and the danger I was placing myself in.

Another glorious new day had dawned, and I decided to spend it exploring the town's marketplace, meandering through the warren of narrow lanes hidden underneath large canvas sheets to shelter from the hot Sahara sun. Countless stalls and open-fronted shops showcased a whole new world of intriguing items that I had never encountered before, and I was fascinated.

My shiny long straight silky hair attracted lots of attention, with many hands stroking it as I meandered through the stalls.

Immediately captivated by a row of beautifully hand woven rugs, I entered the stall to take a closer look and after a short while I noticed two men standing side by side, opposite the stall that I was browsing through. They were not speaking, both had their arms folded, and unlike other Arab men wearing their long gowns, these two men stood apart, dressed in immaculate, western style classy suits and polished shoes. Compared to all the other men I had seen, these two seemed obviously wealthy. I was left wondering why they were standing there together, arms crossed, in silence.

I continued to browse throughout the store, and as time wasn't relevant, I could take all the time I wanted, and I did just that. Having thoroughly checked out every single available item for sale, I strolled out into the lane and entered the next stall. I was having a wonderful time of discovery whilst trying not to be pressured into bargaining by storekeepers desperate to sell me their wares, beckoning me in an unfamiliar language.

After some time I noticed that the two men in suits were again standing like a pair of statues outside, facing my direction. For many hours to follow, every time I moved to a new shop, they moved with me. I had been very careful to pretend not to notice them but kept a vigilant note of what was going on through the corner of my eye. I began to recall the warnings about Western girls disappearing in Morocco, which I had chosen to ignore, and now started wondering if I had been a little naïve to have not taken heed of the warnings.

I had been followed for approximately four hours, and the two men never spoke or made a move to approach me. They just stood outside watching me in silence with their arms folded. It wasn't hard to fathom that I was in some kind of situation, but as to what kind of situation was beyond comprehension. I couldn't speak the language, and no-one seemed to understand English. I didn't know if any of the shopkeepers would even help me, and the reality of my position struck hard. I was a young, naïve girl in a male dominated world, totally under-dressed for the culture and not a woman in sight. I suddenly realized the predicament that I was in and it was not good!

I had managed to continue shopping as though I was not aware that I was being stalked. Meanwhile, every cell in my body was on hyper alert and constantly looking for that illusory escape route.

I finally discovered a possible gateway to freedom in a corner store where, once inside, I noticed a small door near the rear of the shop, opening into a side lane. This wasn't visible from the front due to a row of rugs hanging from the ceiling that blocked the view to the rear of the shop. I decided to stay browsing items at the rear of the shop in readiness for my possible escape. The moment for flight was soon presented when a large group of people slowly walking by, blocked the vision between the two men and the shop, and with a powerful burst of adrenaline I catapulted myself down the side lane and around the next corner like a bolt of lightning.

As I sprinted into the following lane I looked back to see if the two men were in view. Phew! They were nowhere to be seen and I bolted out of sight.

Thankfully I was always a great sprinter and ran as far away as I could, turning many corners until, totally lost and exhausted, I stumbled across a café in a very small narrow lane. Needing to catch my breath I decided it might be a good place to hide out for a while. It had two rooms. One was totally open to the laneway, and the other was hidden from view to the side of it. I sat down at a table in the far corner of the side room and got out my map in the hope of figuring out where I was and how to get back to my accommodation.

Having been followed by these two men for many hours, constantly having to be on alert and then running a marathon had indeed taken a lot out of me. I sat in hiding, sipping many mint teas whilst trying to figure out what to do. After I had rested well, I felt ready to find my way back to my accommodation.

Noticing a small opening in the wall the size of two missing bricks, I decided to take a peek through the gap and to my horror, the two men were standing in silence, with arms crossed, waiting.

I couldn't believe it. How on earth did they know I was there? Had they been informed by some of the locals?

How did they find me? I had run down many lanes and streets to get away. I was both stunned and shocked and now totally concerned for my welfare.

With no back door, no local language skills and nobody to help me. What was I to do? I had nowhere to run.

Realizing that there was no way that I could get rid of these two men, I decided that there was only one thing left for me to do, and that was to confront them.

Facing my fears, I reluctantly resolved that I would go out into the lane, walk up to the two men, who had now been tailing me for approximately five to six hours, and ask them directly, "What do you want from me"?

I took a very deep breath to both calm my nerves and prepare myself emotionally and then harnessed all the courage I could to confront them.

I stepped out into the narrow lane, walked straight up to the two men, stared into their eyes and standing in front of them I took another deep breath and poised to ask the question: "What ...?"

I had only just spoken the first word when from my right, I heard two very familiar drawn-out words:

"Hey, Babe."

It was a moment way beyond belief when I turned to face what, to me, was incomprehensible. "Tim!"

The same Tim that had saved my life in Greece was here, walking straight towards me in this tiny little lane in the middle of Morocco.

This was more than astounding!

"Tim!" I screeched excitedly.

I ran to him like an ecstatic little girl and jumped up with glee. He grabbed me in mid-air and swung me around like a rag doll three times before embracing me.

The two men walked away, and Tim travelled with me throughout Morocco to ensure my safety.

Needless to say, the mystery of "how life worked" had just been stretched again.

How on earth was this possible?

How can the same stranger save me twice? Once behind a bush in Greece, and once again in a small back lane in Morocco?

All I knew about Tim was that he told me that he was a wrestler by trade and lived in Seattle. He was very humble and very physically strong. He was a gentle man and I couldn't imagine him being a wrestler. He never spoke about how he ended up in Morocco.

I was now in my late teens and even more determined to find answers.

I had already come to terms with the realization that we could function as transmitters and receivers, that there existed such a thing as invisible personalities, that our personalities didn't fill up our whole body mass and that our bodies could be utilized by at least two personalities at the same time – but how to explain Tim? How could this happen? Was this the most incredible of coincidences, or were we somehow being watched, monitored, and protected from some kind of other dimension that we can't see?

How is it possible that the same stranger can show up when your life is in danger and save you twice, in different countries, just like that?

I couldn't accept the coincidence theory. It just seemed too incredible to call it a mere coincidence due to the fact that I was in danger in both situations, but what else could it be?

These two events with Tim led me to ponder the possibility of other dimensions existing beyond our scope of awareness from which our lives can be influenced. The question remained. How could this happen?

EVENT 4

I Died on the Wrong Day

I T ALL SEEMED TO happen in slow motion. A collision was unavoidable as an oncoming car, in a moment of poor judgement, cut across our lane in an attempt to make a right-hand turn.

There were no seat belts fitted in those days. We crashed head-on into the oncoming car, and the world started to spin when the car travelling close behind also crashed into us, sending us into yet another spin.

I had terrible pain in my chest and difficulty breathing and began losing consciousness. *The first thought* that registered in my mind as I began to lose consciousness was *"Thank God it is a lovely sunny day!"*

(Many years earlier I had witnessed injured people lying at an accident scene on a cold, wet winter's night, and at the time I thought, *If I ever have a car accident, I hope that it will be on a warm, sunny day.*)

The second thought that came into my mind with confused disbelief was this: *I didn't think that I was meant to die today!* Followed by an instant understanding and awareness that, without a doubt, this was definitely not the correct date of my death, which had already been predetermined.

This was actually the wrong day!

I didn't know which date my death was "set up" for or even how I could possibly know that, but I knew it was definitely the wrong date.

Fascinating!

I was barely conscious when my passenger door opened and my body fell into a man's arm. I could see the palm of his hand

and the light blue neatly pressed cuff of his shirtsleeve as I lost consciousness and collapsed into his arm.

The third thing that happened as I lost consciousness was seeing a film of my life, playing incredibly fast, and even though I couldn't make out any clear pictures due to the sheer speed of it flashing in front of me, I knew that it was a replay of my whole life, running in reverse.

Throughout what seemed just a couple of seconds, the flashing record of my life paused for a split second in three places. The first was the most prominent, when I was about twelve years of age, and two more times when I was much younger. I know that the three events had to do with an internal struggle with my conscience. The "film of my life" had finished, and I instantly understood that everything we do in this life is recorded and that we are somehow accountable for all of our actions.

I am now no longer in my body.

I am invisible and floating about twenty feet above the car. I can see everything and everyone at the scene of the accident below me. It is like a scene or role play in some great drama.

I see the man in the neatly pressed light blue shirt carrying my body to a small grassy traffic island and watch him lay my body down on the grass.

He looks kind and concerned.

I watch many cars moving off the road and parking beside the highway, and I watch people walk over to view my body. I can see many of them holding their fingers and hands over their mouths. Many look as if they are in shock. I know that my body has ceased functioning. I witness the crowd growing in number.

I have a thought: *Where is my boyfriend?*

I scan the crowd below to look for him. I see him walking and stumbling around holding his head between his hands. He is obviously lost, in pain and great shock. No one is looking after him or attending to him. I can see blood running down his face.

I watch with a feeling of compassion for all the people in the drama being played out below. My lifeless body lying on the grass means no more to me than a discarded old jumper, and I have no feeling of attachment to anything happening below. I feel a great love for my boyfriend but do not feel any need to comfort him. I am aware that I am not in the drama anymore, as if I no longer have a role to play in it.

I feel weightless and free, enveloped in a wonderful feeling of bliss and peace that cannot be described in earthly terms.

I continue to watch the drama as yet more people surround my body. There are perhaps thirty or more people staring at my body.

I am able to look at my body objectively. It is a very young and beautiful body with the straightest of shiny, silky long hair.

I look over to my boyfriend again, who is still in shock, and see someone approach him. Then I see a tow truck arrive.

The tow truck parks quickly and awkwardly and the driver hurriedly jumps out and runs across the road to intercept a man sitting in a damaged car nearby.

I can't help but feel the peace and tranquillity of not being in the body anymore. I have no desire to want my body back or to be part of the big drama below ever again, even though my boyfriend is a most wonderful person whom I love deeply and dearly and with whom I am enjoying a good life. None of it ever felt as good as I am feeling now: weightless, invisible, bodiless, free – still myself and as alive as I have ever been, only happier and vastly more peaceful.

I don't want to return.

But then I feel excruciating pain in my chest and find myself in an ambulance. I am back in my body in the drama below, still at the scene of the accident. I see many of the people who surrounded my body now staring into the back of the ambulance.

Two ambulance officers are leaning over me. A large oxygen mask covers my face, and a relieved-looking officer says, "You're going to be all right."

My boyfriend is seated by the rear door and is still in shock. He looks lost. He is covered in blood and has a large cut to his head. We are rushed off to hospital.

Now back in the drama, I feel tightly imprisoned within the confines of my incredibly heavy physical body, in a terrible state of pain, wearing an oxygen mask strapped tightly over my face.

The ambulance officers broke my ribs whilst giving me CPR in order to get my heart beating again.

I roughly work out, from all I saw whilst my body was lifeless on the grass below, that I must have been watching from above for at least eight minutes.

I feel immense loss and disappointment at being back in the drama again.

The next two years left me yearning to depart the restriction of my heavy physical body, and at night on going to bed I would often lie down and silently plead, *Take me, I am ready.* But the next day I would wake up, disappointed to find myself still in the limitations of my physical state.

I eventually accepted my life in the physical, but the experience had changed how I related to life. I could never revert to being the person I was before the experience.

Career and material belongings no longer mattered, and neither did attending parties and having light-hearted polite conversations. Nothing seemed to matter unless it involved deep and meaningful talks about the workings of the universe, and as it was difficult to find people around me who could relate to that, I withdrew into my own thought world, whilst endeavouring to still function in the rest of the world surrounding me.

By now I had experienced enough to understand that human life presented far greater capabilities than what we are led to believe. At the time of this event, the medical profession generally believed that if you were clinically dead for more than four minutes, you would have permanent brain damage. I had learnt from my own experience that that belief was absolutely not accurate.

I also knew that what I had witnessed could not possibly have been seen from within my deceased body, as has been suggested by many in the medical fraternity.

I no longer feared death and can even say that I welcome and look forward to it. I feel fortunate and privileged to have had the experience of my life without the body during this lifetime.

At this stage in my physical journey, life as a "human being" was proving to be far more interesting than what we generally believe it to be.

We can transmit and receive information much like radios and televisions.

More than one personality can share a physical body at the same time.

But how does Tim, who saved me from imminent danger twice, fit in?

I also now fully understood that we don't die.

The questions of the "life recording" still remained. Who or what is doing the recording? How does that fit in with our life?

With a great passion to find the pieces of life's jigsaw puzzle forever growing within me, I was now fully committed to figuring this out, and nothing in my life would be more important than that. I had seen that there was "more", and I had an unquenchable desire to understand it.

EVENT 5

A Haunted House and a Beautiful Being of Light

L IKE MOST KIDS ON camping trips, I endured many scary ghost stories. These stories were always seen as a joke rather than to be taken seriously. I never thought for a moment that I would one day have my own *real* scary ghost story to tell!

Living in London, I had come home from work and switched on the TV to catch the daily BBC news. To my surprise there was a news story about a house that had become "haunted", with TV crew filming objects being thrown "by nothing visible" from one side of the room to the other. The footage lasted only a couple of minutes before the reporter and camera crew ran out of the house carrying their equipment.

I was stunned. This was the normal daily BBC news, and I couldn't imagine that, had this happened in Australia, it would have been given any attention at all, let alone have a TV crew go out to capture the event!

You could clearly see objects being yanked off the walls and thrown around, but there wasn't anyone to be seen who was doing the throwing.

More questions invaded my thoughts:

How is this possible? How can something totally invisible be throwing heavy material objects around? The physical proof of this was there for everyone to see. But why couldn't we physically see what was actually throwing the objects around? Why could our eyes not see this?

My logical mind couldn't grasp what I had seen, and I was left with a barrage of questions to contemplate.

I left London and returned to Australia, where, a few years later, I had my own frightening haunted house ghost story to live through.

I was in my early twenties and preparing for college. I had found an old Edwardian house with unbelievably cheap rent just a five-minute drive from the college I was attending. It was detached so that you could walk right around the house, and it had a private driveway along one side. It was ideal and having two bedrooms meant that I could share the rent and live very cheaply. I rented a room to another student and her pet cat of seven years. We moved in, and the cat confidently took over all the best spots, as cats do.

One day, not long after we had settled in, my new flatmate and I were having a chat in the lounge room whilst the cat lay in a sunny spot on the table next to the open window. Suddenly our conversation was interrupted by the loud hissing noise of the cat. Immediately, Jane and I snapped to attention and turned to see the cat standing with it's back highly arched, all four legs drawn together, hairs standing on end like spikes, staring and hissing aggressively and intensely at something. We both turned to see what the cat was staring at, but there was nothing there to see.

Jane and I looked at each other, confused as to what was going on with the cat. We watched the cat hiss again in the same direction and then spring out of the room through the open window as if his life depended on it.

Jane conveyed that in the seven years that she had lived with her cat, he had always been placid, and she had never seen him behave in that manner. It was two weeks before her beloved cat reappeared.

A month went by and all seemed well until the same scenario was repeated: the cat again arched his back, hissed violently at something, and, with hairs on end, vanished in a flash through the open window. This time, sadly for my flatmate, her beloved cat had deserted us forever. It was never to be seen again.

About a month later, home alone in the lounge room, I heard loud, desperate, frantic knocking at the front door. Thinking that someone must be hurt or that something terrible had happened, I called, "I'm coming, I'm coming," and stepped into the long wood-floored passageway leading to the front door – but something was not quite right in the picture in front of me. The top half of the door had a large frosted glass window, and when someone stood at the door, you could see a silhouette. I was still hearing the loud, frantic knocking, but there was no silhouette to be seen.

"OK, I'm coming!" I yelled. Even though I couldn't see anyone standing there, my ears were definitely hearing the sounds of someone frantically knocking. *How odd, yet there must be someone there*, I thought. *Maybe it's a small child?* I was still trying to figure out why I couldn't see a silhouette as I approached the door. *Not possible; it's too loud and strong to be a child*, I concluded.

Again assuring the one desperately knocking, "I'm coming, I'm coming!", I approached the front door. With my hand on the door handle, there was still no silhouette of any kind, only the persistent knocking.

The knocking ceased the instant I pulled the door towards me. I stood totally dumbfounded. Nobody was there.

An icy coldness passed through my body, as if for a moment I was inside a freezer, and yet it was a perfectly still and sunny summer's day.

Confused, I explored outside. I checked the front of the house, went out to the footpath, and looked in both directions. Then I walked around the house to see if I could find someone, but there was nobody. *That's weird*, I thought to myself.

My rational mind jumped into action trying to figure this out, but I was unable to find a logical explanation. For sanity's sake, I concluded that it must have been some kind of prank and that I just couldn't work out the logical answer at this time.

When my flatmate returned, I shared what had happened. She too concluded that there must be a logical answer, and we just couldn't see it.

Nothing untoward happened over the next few weeks, and life continued as usual.

Some weeks later, home alone, reading peacefully in the lounge room, I heard a loud noise in the hallway. I immediately sat up erect, fully at attention. "What was that?" My ears pricked up to listen;

Klonk-klonk, klonk-klonk, klonk-klonk ....

Someone was inside the house! It sounded as if a big, heavy man, wearing hard, unbending army boots, was trudging down the hall towards the lounge room. Each step was the same: first what sounded like the heel of a solid boot connecting heavily with the wooden floor, followed a second later by the rest of the boot slapping down on the floor.

There was no mistaking what the sound represented. The more I heard, the more convinced I was that someone big and heavy was definitely walking on the wooden floor of the hallway and coming closer with each step.

I froze and held my breath. There was someone inside the house!

Both front and back doors were locked, and the front windows didn't open. Even if I *was* mistaken about the door being locked, I would have heard this person walk up the wooden steps and onto the porch before trying to get in through the front door. I also knew that it wasn't my flatmate's walk and that I would have heard her keys. The walking had started inside the house! How was that possible?

I looked up at the lounge room door as the footsteps came closer. It was a small comfort that the lounge room door, even though not lockable, was closed. I had no idea what to expect. I held my breath and watched in nervous anticipation.

Would it come all the way down to the lounge room? Was the lounge room doorknob going to turn?

The window in the lounge room was open and I had thoughts of bounding through it like the cat. Instead, I just sat there like a lump of concrete, unable to move.

I was hardly breathing, and my mind was again doing overtime! Whatever it was, kept on coming.

Klonk-klonk, klonk-klonk, klonk-klonk ....

Whoever or whatever this was had now passed the front bedroom door and was passing the second bedroom door. The lounge room door was next. I still couldn't move, and my heart was racing!

Klonk-klonk, klonk-klonk, klonk-klonk ....

The footsteps were continuing down the middle of the wide wooden hallway. When they reached as far as the lounge room, the next step turned and came straight towards the door. The following step did exactly the same! I was now completely frozen in fear. Clearly, something or someone big and heavy was standing right outside, facing the lounge room door, and I couldn't even do the cat thing!

A heavy, eerie silence pervaded the house. Unable to move, I watched the doorknob to see if it would turn. Thankfully it didn't. My heart was beating so fast that I wondered whether I might have a heart attack and instantly knew it was possible to die of fright.

Whatever was on the other side of the door was not going anywhere, it seemed. Nor was I, for that matter. My heart still pounding, I tried my best to stay calm, and so I sat for many hours, hoping my flatmate would come home. She might not, as she spent many nights away, either at her parents or her boyfriend's places, so unfortunately for me in this house, I was often home alone.

Thankfully, I heard her car pull up. I hadn't moved for what seemed an eternity, and although I wanted to warn her, I couldn't move. I heard her walk up the creaky steps to the porch, cross it and unlock the door, go to her room and drop her bags, walk down the hallway, and come into the lounge room, as if nothing unusual was going on!

All was perfectly normal again.

Questions pierced my mind:

What happened to whatever it was that had stopped at the lounge room door? Had I gone mad? There was obviously nothing there now!

I explained what had happened, and Jane was convinced that there was always a logical explanation for everything and that one day it would be found. As I couldn't find an answer myself and I was desperate for one, I decided that her response was comforting and reassuring. Although not totally convinced, I adopted the same stance and went into as much denial as I could manage, and life went back to normal.

At least for a few weeks, until one afternoon I'd gone home from college for lunch. Whilst making my sandwich, I had a creepy feeling that someone was staring straight at me from very close behind me. I instantly turned around, but there was nobody there. I returned to making my sandwich, but the uneasiness remained, and I quickly grabbed my sandwich and left to return to college.

I shared my experiences with a colleague who surprised me by her non-judgemental acceptance of my experiences.

"I live in an old farmhouse, and our family share it with a little old lady who lived there before she passed away. We all experience her moving around the house," she explained.

Wow! Relief! It wasn't just happening to me! I had found a person who not only accepted what I was relating but even had some experiences of her own.

"Are you ever afraid"? I asked.

"Oh no, she's a gentle lady, and we all feel her gentleness. None of us fear her."

She was so lucky, I thought. Whatever or whoever it was in the house where I lived, definitely couldn't be described that way at all. If I had to describe the feeling that I got from its presence, I would say it was aggressive, angry, determined, resentful, and possibly even dangerous.

I shared how I was feeling uncomfortable being home alone and that my flatmate was away a lot.

"Why not go to the spiritualist church and ask for help?" she suggested.

I had never heard of a spiritualist church but was desperate for help, so I took her advice and was given contact details.

I rocked up to the church at their next meeting, and that was an experience in itself. I had never been exposed to people channelling spirits before, and I felt way out of my depth. After the meeting was over, I introduced myself and explained my situation. They were very happy to assist.

The spiritualist church helpers arrived at my place as promised and walked both around and through the house whilst I made refreshments. They seemed to be doing a lot of talking to someone throughout the house.

After the inspection was over, we sat down for refreshments, and they gave me their findings.

"You have a very angry and unhappy male presence in this house who has lived here for many years before you arrived. He doesn't want any more intruders in his house and wants you to leave." She repeated, "He sees you as an intruder and wants you out."

She went on, "You will need to convince him that he has passed over and that he needs to move toward the light. Whenever you feel his presence, you will need to tell him that he no longer has a body and needs to move on from here."

She added, "You might want to consider moving out of this house altogether as this is a strong and angry spirit. Due to the upset nature of this spirit and your own inexperience in dealing with such matters, it would be our advice that you consider that option."

I felt their uneasiness in the house throughout their visit, and I could see that they were obviously looking forward to getting out.

After much advice as to how to best handle this should I decide to stay, they departed. It didn't take long before the chance to use their advice had presented itself.

I was confronted once again with loud, frantic knocking at the front door, and I looked down the hall to see no silhouette through the frosted glass. I decided to ignore it, but the knocking got louder and even more aggressive and angry. Not knowing what to expect if I didn't open the door at all and risked greater anger, I decided to open the door to ease the situation. Another icy cold shiver went straight through my body as I stood with the door ajar and nobody there.

One could not be blamed for wondering why at this stage I didn't move out. I should have, but I came from an overly proud and rather stubborn line of ancestors who just wouldn't be beaten, including my mother. If I dared to run home from school when I was young, saying that someone had hit me, she would send me straight back to hit them even harder. There were no cowards to be had in our family.

So here I was – too proud to go running and too stubborn to move out. If anyone was moving out, it wasn't going to be me! I was very frustrated that my flatmate hadn't experienced anything other than the two cat experiences and that the experiences seemed only to take place when I was home alone.

Over the following months these events became a regular occurrence. I would use the advice given by the spiritualist church and address whatever this thing was, in a kind but stern voice, with compassion, trying to explain that it needed to leave this earthly plane for the next one where it belonged. I suspected that this thing could probably move through closed doors if it wanted to, as it had no body of physical matter, but it probably thought that it was still human and therefore couldn't. I also thought that if I could prove this, it might finally depart.

Although I felt a bit ridiculous, whenever I felt its presence, I would say things like: "You are no longer limited as a human being, and you can prove that to yourself by walking through doors. Physical bodies can't do that, but you will be able to, and then you might understand that you are totally free to go anywhere in the universe; you don't need to be stuck here anymore. You just need to go towards the light, and you will be freed from all the hurt that you have experienced."

No matter how hard I tried, nothing worked, and whatever this thing was, it was breaking down my nerves. My inner strength to deal with these events was waning, and my hands had starting shaking nervously whenever I heard it walk or felt its presence nearby. I had reached a point where I was now afraid to stay in the house alone and fled to stay with my boyfriend at his mother's place in order to recoup my strength.

After a couple of weeks' rest I bravely decided to return home. Thankfully my boyfriend offered to come and stay for a week to make sure that I would be OK.

Nothing unusual happened during my boyfriend's stay, and I finally thought that life might return to normal and all would be well. My boyfriend returned to his own home and I was ready to dive into my studies.

On my first night alone again I woke in the middle to the all-too-familiar sound of heavy, aggressive footsteps klonking down the hallway.

My heart jumped a beat. This had never happened at night before! *Why didn't this happen while my boyfriend was staying here? Why now on the first night that I am all alone again?* I shook nervously, and I wasn't mentally able to handle this anymore!

Why always only when I am here alone? I thought, and the possibility suddenly struck me that this thing might have been targeting me to break down my strength for some kind of agenda aimed obviously at me, and that I might be in real danger.

I could also sense that there was more than just the usual heaviness in the atmosphere. I could see how my strength had been worn down. And clearly this entity was getting stronger, louder, and more determined with every event.

Was this thing building up to some kind of climax? If so, what?

I was afraid like never before. My heart pounded. The awful thought then struck me as I remembered the BBC TV news of the haunted house and how, after many days, they had to call in an old retired priest to exorcise the house, who earlier in his life had carried out many exorcisms on people whose bodies had been taken over by spirits.

Is that what this thing has in mind?

My nerves weren't up to this anymore.

My bedroom door was closed, as it had now become a habit to always keep every door closed.

Klonk-klonk, klonk-klonk, klonk-klonk ....

In the past it had always walked down to the lounge room door, and I was hoping it would continue going past my bedroom door, stopping at the lounge as usual. I could hardly breathe!

Klonk-klonk, klonk-klonk ....

The last two steps had turned to face my bedroom door. *It* knew where I was, and *it* was right outside my bedroom! I held my breath. *Will* it *come through the door?*

Although I was petrified, I kept remembering my grandmother's words about how we were a tough breed. I knew that I had to be strong and cope. I also knew that it had never walked through a closed door, which gave me some comfort.

I knew that I was losing my emotional strength and that I was now a nervous wreck who had no skills for dealing with this. What good was school if it didn't teach you to handle life situations like this?

I felt as though the night would never end!

The sun began to shine and a new day was beginning. I decided not to open the bedroom door until I really had to start getting ready for college and grabbed a book to read, trying to settle my mind. I had even contemplated going out through the bedroom window but decided that I needed a shower, and my mother's words, "Don't be a coward! You go back and fight", were forever hammered and stuck inside my brain.

I eventually plucked up the courage to open the bedroom door. All was well again. I showered, went to college, and was ever so grateful for the beautiful sunny day ahead to strengthen me.

Although I had stopped going home for lunch breaks, I needed to go back to pick something up for afternoon class, so reluctantly I headed home.

I opened the front door to see my flatmate standing frozen, like a white marble statue, in the middle of the hallway. Her face was very pale, and I understood immediately that Jane had finally had an encounter of her own. For me, that was a great relief. *Finally it has happened to someone else!* I felt immense compassion for her.

I placed my hands on her face saying, "It's OK. You're OK", and led her to the lounge, attentively closing the hall door behind us as we entered. I sat her down on the couch. "I'll make us both a cup of tea," and I left her sitting in silence to give her time to relax again. Thankfully the kitchen was a small room off the lounge room so we didn't need to open the hallway door.

When I returned with a cup of tea, she was starting to come out of her stark and rigid, stare-into-nothingness gaze, and a bit of colour was returning to her face. I handed her a cup of tea, but her hands were too shaky, so I had to grab it back and put it down on the coffee table.

"What happened?" I asked

Her mouth fell open as if she were about to tell me something, but nothing came out. Her eyes were still glazed and hadn't been able to connect properly with mine, and I could see that she was still in shock but was going to be OK.

I dropped any questioning, sat back, and sipped my tea, allowing her whatever time she needed to get a hold of herself.

After a few minutes, she slowly turned and looked straight into my eyes. I was relieved to see that she was back to normal although obviously shaken. Jane then began to explain what had happened;

"I was walking down the hall to go to my room, and something started bashing the wall right next to me! It was as if someone was really angry and was out of control and was bashing the wall as hard as he could with his fists. I know how this sounds, and it is really weird, but I didn't imagine it! It was right next to me, but I couldn't see anything! I was definitely not imagining it! It happened! But there wasn't anyone there! I was really frightened and scared, and I didn't know what to do. I just froze over. It was horrible, and I was petrified! I couldn't breathe properly. It was so frightening!" Her explanation amused me somewhat, as it was obvious that she was trying to convince me to believe that her experience was very real and that she wasn't mad or making it up. As if I needed convincing!

Her experience did intrigue me, though. Bashing on the wall? That was different. I had never experienced that one before. However, the anger part was definitely consistent. I had only experienced loud heavy walking to whatever room I was in, loud and aggressive knocking on the front door with no silhouette, freezing cold sensations going through my body, and the feeling of being stared at by nobody. Jane's experience baffled me.

Why did it bash the wall on the only occasion when I wasn't there?

My flatmate was too terrified to stay and decided to move out with all of her belongings, less one cat. Her front bedroom with the bay window that overlooked the street was now without curtains, empty and deserted. The approach through the front yard to the house no longer looked homely and inviting.

I couldn't bear to stay in the house on my own the night that Jane moved out, so I drove for a couple of hours to my parents' house in the country to get some respite for a few days before returning. It was certainly a great relief to get some distance between myself, and the house. I even wondered if I was brave enough to go back at all.

This beautiful and very cheap Edwardian house had turned into a living nightmare. I wondered if this had happened to the previous tenants and if that was the reason why this house was so cheap.

But what was I to make of the uncharacteristic bashing on the wall?

So many baffling questions floated through my mind.

After a stint at my parents' house and still needing more respite, I drove to my boyfriend's place for another stint of respite with my boyfriend and his mother, I stayed with them until I felt that I had regained enough strength to return home.

It was late evening when I arrived home. The dark, empty front room gave an unwelcome feeling as I walked up to the front porch. The steps and wooden boards squeaked as I approached the front door, and I already regretted coming home.

It would have made a good scene in a horror movie as the air of creepiness prevailed. *I must be crazy to have come back here alone*, I thought to myself.

I turned the key and opened the door. My stomach was almost turning inside out. Quickly I ran to switch on the lights near the door and made straight for my bedroom. I closed the door to my bedroom and decided to go straight to sleep. It was one of the few days in my life when I failed to brush my teeth before sleeping. The strength that I thought I had gained whilst away had dissipated into nothingness. I had completely lost my nerve, and I knew that I was devoid of any emotional strength.

I woke up in the middle of the night with a strong but gentle, penetrating sensation of movement in the middle of my forehead, just above and in between my eyebrows.

It felt in width somewhat in between a ten- and a twenty-cent coin.

I opened my eyes and could not believe what I was looking at.

A soft yellowy golden glow permeated the space in my room, and a being of bright yellowy white light stood facing me at the foot of my bed. We were connected by a very bright laser-like beam of light coming from the light being's forehead and penetrating straight into my own forehead.

I was staring at this thing in absolute wonderment. *What on earth is this? Am I dreaming?*

I moved up into a sitting position with my back pressed against my bedhead, and all the while the beam stayed connected to the same spot on my forehead. I was now sitting bolt upright in my bed and had no idea what this thing was that I was looking at. I had never heard of anything like this before, and I certainly hadn't been taught about this at school. I had zero understanding of what was occurring.

Surprisingly, I was not at all afraid, and I was incredibly in awe.

For a long time I sat bolt upright, staring at this beautiful being or whatever it was at the foot of my bed. I could feel that this light being was giving me more love than I could ever have imagined possible, with such intensity that it simply cannot be expressed in the English language.

Not only did I feel incredibly loved, I felt immensely cared for. I knew that I was safe and that I was somehow being nurtured, looked after, and assisted. My own energy and strength had been terribly depleted over the months of living in this house, and I felt as if I was being replenished and my energy was being restored. I knew at that time, without any doubt whatsoever, that I was being charged up just like a battery.

The sensation of energy moving into my body through where the beam of light connected to my forehead was constant throughout the whole encounter. The beam was the brightest light in the room, and its intensity was most probably due to it being the most concentrated and intensified area of energy.

This being of light had the shape of a smallish person, perhaps my shoulder height of around 140 cm or around four feet five inches tall, and although I couldn't see through it due to its intense light, I could see that it was not solid. It was not of physical matter. It was only light, and yet I also knew that it had an intelligence far superior to my own. I knew that, compared to this light being, I was very limited.

There was a hint of arms down either side of the figure, but they were not clearly defined. If I had to draw its shape I would draw a thinner area of light at the neck and a slightly elongated head with a thinning of light where we would expect a pair of eyes to be.

There was no hint of a nose or mouth at all.

I have no real idea as to how long this encounter went on, but at a guess I would say that I stared at this being of light and was being energized by it for approximately fifteen minutes.

Still staring at this being of light and having a feeling that I was now fully charged and energised, the feeling of movement in my forehead gently ceased, and I watched the bright white beam retract into the being of light, which took approximately four slow seconds.

I continued to stare at this being in amazement. I felt totally loved and nurtured by it.

Slowly, the being of light began to fade away. It didn't move away. It just faded away, and I was left alone, fully awake and fully recharged like a brand-new battery! Any thought of lying down and going back to sleep was totally out of the question. I felt "electric" and spent all night rejoicing in this amazing encounter. The love that I had received was way beyond any love I had ever known. I felt amazingly blessed to have had this encounter, and I was left wondering if anyone else on earth had ever had this amazing experience and how I could possibly even begin to explain it to others, let alone expect people to believe me.

It was indeed another "wow" moment in my life and certainly not what I had expected might happen that night.

A week went by without incident, and I hoped that, whatever that being of light was, it might have somehow freed the house of that other thing that had caused havoc on my nerves and sent the cat and my flatmate running.

I was amazed at how well I slept over that week, and finally I thought that life might be back to normal again. Then one night I woke and glanced at the clock to see that it was 4.00 a.m.

I headed to the bathroom and closed the door, as closing doors had become a habit in that house, and I sat on the toilet. I picked up a book from the floor and began to read when I heard *Klonk-klonk, klonk-klonk, klonk-klonk* …. This time the footsteps sounded more determined than ever before. I had the distinct feeling that this time it was different. It was on a mission, and it started at the front door and was coming all the way down the hallway passing the two bedrooms, the lounge room, and was now heading straight for the bathroom.

"Frightened" does not come close to describe how I was feeling. It had never walked all the way to the bathroom before, and the bathroom was the only room in the house without a window to escape through.

For some reason I just knew this was the "grand finale". I knew by the way it was walking, and I also knew without doubt that something huge was about to happen. I could hardly breathe! Again, I froze in fear.

Klonk-klonk, klonk-klonk, klonk-klonk ….

Then the last two steps turned to face the bathroom door: *klonk-klonk* ….

It was standing outside the bathroom, facing the door. I had a sense that it knew that I could not escape and that I also knew a major event was about to take place. A final showdown was about to happen, and I had no idea of what to expect or how to handle it. I felt threatened and in danger.

I sat there for a long time trying to figure out what I could do, but there was no manhole in the bathroom and no window to break through.

My bottom was getting numb from sitting for so long. I finished up, dressed, and stood just inside the door, petrified. Should I open it?

I could feel its heavy presence and remembered my grandmother's words: "We're as tough as a bunch of weeds, and weeds don't die easily."

With those words in mind, I mustered up all my courage and opened the bathroom door.

What happened next will be very hard to believe!

Within a millisecond, I cannot breathe. It feels as if I have been hit by a freight train at full speed, and I am squashed against the bathroom wall with my feet dangling. I am gasping for air, and my lungs are squashed inwards. Interestingly, it feels as if an invisible metal plate, the size and shape of my lungs, is holding me flat against the wall with incredible strength. The rest of my body did not feel affected.

I am in total panic, as I can't get any air into my lungs. I move my hand to the doorframe and grab the architrave. It is all I can do. Pinned to the wall, my lungs still squashed, I am frightened that I might lose consciousness if I don't get any air. I can't breathe. I am gasping for air, and all of a sudden I am released and fall to the floor. I sense that something else is also in the room and has pulled *it* off my body. Something has helped me.

I ran down the hall, grabbing my car keys and in the darkness of the night, I fled that house as fast as I possibly could. I never spent another night in that house again. My father came with me to pick up all of my belongings, and I finally moved out.

Many questions remained, and I wanted answers. I wanted to know the truth of how the world worked, how these events were possible, why these were not part of everyday normal discussions, and why nothing about these types of events was ever studied at school.

After collecting my belongings, I went to the real estate agent to explain that I had vacated the property and that I would not be returning. To my surprise he said, "Just like all the others. No notice, and almost six months to the day. At least you've been polite enough to let me know; thanks."

I was dumbfounded by his remark. "What do you mean?" I asked.

He went on to tell me that although the lease had always been for twelve months, no one had stayed longer than six months in the last two years even though they lowered the rent substantially, and all tenants had left without giving notice.

I told him without going into particulars that I believed the house to be haunted. He didn't seem surprised by my comment, but he didn't seem to want to discuss it. He thanked me for at least letting him know, and we dropped the subject.

His comments regarding previous tenants intrigued me, so I decided to ask some questions around the neighbourhood to see what I could find out. Most people I asked didn't know anything, but I approached an elderly lady who had lived in the area most of her life. According to her there had been a death in the house a couple of years before, which was either a suicide or a murder.

After moving out, I occasionally had to drive past the house as it was on a main thoroughfare. Each time I saw a different for-sale sign on the front fence.

About ten years after I had moved out, I was driving past the house and noticed another for-sale sign displayed on the fence. Intrigued to speak to someone now living in the house a decade later, I decided to stop and brave a knock on the door to introduce myself and find out.

Even after ten years, it took a bit of courage to walk down that path, up the wooden steps, and onto the porch and knock. Whilst waiting for someone to answer the door, I saw black smoke residue on the top architrave of the door as if a candle had been burnt there regularly. No answer.

I wondered if anyone was home. I knocked again and decided to wait a little longer.

I had heard a noise inside so I knocked gently a third time. Finally there was movement in the hallway and I could see shapes coming towards me through the frosted glass window of the door.

What happened next rather surprised me;

Usually when you knock on a door, one person opens the door. In this instance, the door opened, and I was faced with a family of three. Wow! That was a first.

I introduced myself to a Greek middle-aged couple and a girl perhaps eight years of age who was standing between them.

"Hi, my name is Viviana, and I lived in this house ten years ago. I had many unusual events in this house and I was wondering if you had any unusual events happen here as well?"

My question was obviously not welcome, and the man instantly retorted, "No! Nothing bad ever happen here!"

To which the woman echoed, "No, nothing bad here."

Interesting. I hadn't asked if something bad had happened. I only asked if they had had unusual events! They seemed edgy, and I could see by their reactions that they were not comfortable. Before the man closed the door, I leaned down to the young girl and asked, "What do you think of this house?"

She cringed, lifting both closed fists to hide her mouth. "It's scary." The look on her face told all.

The woman then pushed the little girl behind her and said, "She don't know nothing." They quickly closed the door.

I guess I couldn't expect them to tell me anything. They were, after all, trying to sell the house. But the little girl's answer was all the confirmation I needed. The house was still "haunted" ten years later.

I felt sorry for the Greek couple and the little girl. Who knows what they had to endure? Whatever was haunting that house was probably a lot angrier now. No wonder all three were standing united in emotional support to open that door!

I had been in my early twenties when I had lived in that house and it had certainly added to my growing intrigue as to how life worked.

I had already experienced that humans were capable of being transmitters and receivers and deduced logically that humans must have the capacity and the capability of developing telepathy through somehow intercepting invisible wavelengths just like radios and TVs. I also experienced that invisible personalities existed and that they were certainly as much alive as I was.

I had also been shown that our personality didn't fill up our whole body entirely because I had briefly experienced that two personalities could share one body at the same time.

In the case of Tim showing up and saving me from danger in two different countries I was left pondering the possibility of other dimensions existing from which our lives can be influenced and possibly intercepted.

My death experience taught me that we live beyond the physical body and that our lives are somehow recorded. But who or what is doing the recording?

The haunted house and the "being of light" experience left even more questions. I had to conclude that humans were not only made of solid physical matter, but that we are also made of energy. Having witnessed that an intelligent being of light existed, I was left with the question "Where did it come from?"

But what of the haunting entity that I could hear walking and not see?

I knew that dogs hear sounds beyond the pitch of humans, so we know that sounds exist that we humans are not able to hear. Dog whistles are proof enough.

The cat intensely focused its stare at something that my flatmate and I could not see, so as human beings, we are limited in our ability to register everything that is going on around us. There is so much more going on in our world and we seem to be oblivious to it.

But being squashed by something invisible? How can something that appears to have no solid physical substance, physically squash a physical being? I just couldn't grasp that one at all. How does that work?

I still had so much to figure out.

EVENT 6

Time Splits

A FTER I LEFT THE haunted house behind me, life seemed pretty normal. I travelled overseas again, settled and worked in Amsterdam for a while, and eventually returned to Australia.

Many years had passed since I had bolted out of the haunted house, and nothing greatly untoward had happened during those years.

I was now in my late twenties and had taken the job of swimming pool manager at the Traralgon City Pool. It was the summer of the devastating Ash Wednesday bushfires in which many people lost their lives, and it was one of the hottest summers on record at the time.

There had been an eight-day heat wave with no escape from the soaring heat. During these days, the pool became overcrowded, and it was a daunting task to secure patron safety. One particularly hot day placed a great deal of strain on both myself and staff members. It was impossible to see the bottom of the pool through the huge numbers of people cooling off in the water, and there was a queue at least thirty meters long outside of the entry gate still wanting to come in.

I had made the difficult decision to not allow any more patrons to enter the pool premises for safety reasons. I walked outside along the queue of people waiting at the entry gate, advising them to either go home or go to a nearby river to cool off. Though they were clearly disappointed, I was thankful for their understanding, and all departed to cool off elsewhere.

Back by the poolside, I noticed two boys I had already spoken to twice in regard to the dangers of what they were doing, and here they were doing it again! I had already saved one girl from the bottom of the pool and had another rushed to hospital. After eight days of scorching heat and constant stress I had reached breaking point. It was the most stressful working day of my life.

I snapped.

I must have looked like a madwoman. I blew that whistle until I was red in the face. The whole pool sprang to attention. The boys turned to look at me, knowing that they had been caught again and I could see the fear on their faces.

I started to bolt towards them like a big mean bull, who had just been waved an enormous red flag. They scrambled out of the pool, grabbed their towels, and bolted towards the exit for their escape.

I had completely lost the plot. After a week of intense stress and incredible responsibility for people's safety, my ability to cope was gone, and I really had reached breaking point. I was furious and about to take all my tension out on these two most unfortunate boys.

So there I was, now with everyone's attention, in my bikini, running at cyclone speed, my whistle flying behind me, bolting to the exit. I grabbed an arm of each boy, and with a steel grip, I marched them to the office, determined to make sure that they never did that again! I pushed them through the open door and literally flung them to the other side of the room as if I had the strength of twenty. I really had lost the plot.

The boys, now flung against the opposite wall, stared at me with fear written all over their faces, as if I was about to murder them. In a moment of grace, I was suddenly shocked at this scenario.

Then something extraordinary occurred: I was *no longer inside my body*. I was looking down from the ceiling height, above where my body was standing just inside the doorway. The scene below was frozen in time.

I look at the scene below. The boys are obviously frightened. The "I" that is now up above and bodiless is looking down at this out-of-control frozen scene. I look at my body and silently say to myself: *Look at this scene, Viviana; these boys are petrified. Get ahold of yourself.*

Another moment passes as if frozen in time as I absorb the state of the scene below. Then I find myself back in my body, now looking calmly and clearly at the two boys in front of me, still frozen in fear. I hear the voice of my lifeguard as he enters the room from behind me and says, "What is going on?"

Time is suddenly unfrozen again, and we are all back in normal time.

I thankfully and calmly reply; "Can you deal with this please? I need ten minutes out."

I leave the room and retreat to my private office where I lock the door, sit at my desk, and cry for ten minutes until I feel all stress has left my body. I return to my work with renewed capacity to handle whatever I am faced with.

After this experience, I started to wonder what "personality" was.

Looking down at my deceased body in the earlier car accident, I could see that it was lifeless, and yet the motivated feeling of who I was, my personality, had survived. Although invisible – I was no longer "wearing" my body – I was very much alive and observing everything that was happening below. I was no more attached to my body than being attached to an old jumper that had simply worn out.

But in that scenario, I was deceased.

In this scenario, however, I was still very much alive, my body had just frozen in time. The very essence of who I thought I was, my personality, had moved out of my physical body and time as we understand it, was split into two different time frames. Time continued as my personality looked down, advising me to look at my behaviour in the frozen scene below where time had stopped.

Time had split away from normal everyday reality, and time itself now carried a huge question mark. My brain was well and truly being stretched all over again.

Through my experiences I was able to understand that 'personality' is capable of departing the body, whether the body is deceased or still very much alive.

The events that I had so far endured taught me that we are made up of more than just a physical body. Our physical body is only just a part of what we are. It is certainly not all of what we are. Through all of my experiences so far, I can only conclude that we function in a multitude of ways. We function in a physical sense but also with frequencies, wavelengths and light energy and that we have an innate ability to both transmit and receive information.

I contemplated whether we might even have our own individual frequency just as the physical body has its own individual fingerprint.

I had certainly witnessed that life was definitely a lot more than just a mortal physical body.

EVENT 7

An Out-of-Body Experience

O F ALL OF MY outside-the-box events, this is one of my most memorable experiences, and it took place in the same year, not long after my swimming pool experience.

One glorious sunny day, my boyfriend and I were driving through the gentle undulating hills surrounding Yallourn North. We were both feeling wonderfully content and peaceful and enjoying the quiet spaces of our own thoughts as we took in the beauty surrounding us.

Bright yellow daisies amongst fresh green pastures rolled past my passenger window when all of a sudden I had gone blind.

I had lost my eyesight!

Shock was my initial response, followed by confusion. My eyes were wide open, yet there was nothing but white in the scene before me. There was no picture. There was no scene to be seen. There was just white.

My inquisitive mind kicked in immediately with the question *How come I am seeing white and not black?* I had assumed, wrongly or rightly, that if someone were blind, they would see not light but rather darkness, as if with eyes closed.

Before I could figure this out, a large white rectangle began to appear in my vision and a second question entered my mind: *What is that?* The white rectangle began to shrink and got smaller and smaller.

Whilst frantically searching for a logical answer in my mind, I suddenly became aware that I was looking down at the roof of the car in which I was a passenger! The body of the car was a deep olive green, but the roof of the car was white.

I could see logically what was happening, but *how* it was happening was impossible to explain. Yet again, my mind was thrown a new challenge.

Within what seemed like a fraction of a second from the time that I first thought that I had gone blind, I had somehow travelled through the roof of the car, and I was no longer in my physical body. There was no sensation of weight at all, other than a gentle *whoosh* sound as I moved higher and higher.

Almost at once I could see the surrounding hills from above. I could also see the car travelling along the road below, and it was now the size of a matchbox and getting smaller. I continued higher and higher, and the soft *whoosh* sound accompanied me as I ascended. I saw the township of Yallourn North. Still higher, the neighbouring towns of Moe, Morwell, and Traralgon came into view, and even higher I began to see the greater part of Latrobe Valley, the Streszlecki Ranges, and beyond. I continued to rise until the horizon was no longer a straight line and began to seemingly curve away at the left and right sides of my vision, and the curvature of the earth took shape before my eyes.

This all happened within a moment in time, the *whoosh* sound accompanying me throughout the experience. I had travelled approximately a kilometre upwards. I had no weight and no body, yet I felt no different in my personality.

It happened so fast that initially there was a moment of confusion. Then came the thought *Where am I going?* and as I ascended further and further the earth started to curve into a globe, I panicked, and fear took over: *Oh my God! What is happening to me? Where am I going?*

I became totally panic stricken, and as soon as I was taken over by fear, I went into immediate reverse and whooshed back down to earth, through the white roof of the car, and back into my body.

With a great sigh of relief I acknowledged that I was back in my body once again, but I was left forever wondering: where would I have gone and what would I have experienced, if I hadn't become so fearful?

So, as many times before, I was in that all-too-familiar mind-set of wanting answers and desperately trying to make sense of everything for the sake of my sanity and my logical intelligence. As always, I was frustrated that there was nowhere to turn for answers.

What am I? Who am I? Where did I come from? What does it mean to be human?

And even more frustratingly, *Why doesn't anyone want to talk about this stuff?*

I looked over to my boyfriend to see if he had noticed anything during my ordeal, but he was just in the same peaceful state as before, as if nothing had happened. I knew that this was not something I could discuss with him, and as usual, I stayed silent and once again felt very alone and isolated. I desperately wanted to share these amazing experiences, but I had learnt that it was best not to.

I was now in my late twenties and I had already learnt some fascinating things about life as a human such as the fact that our physical bodies are nothing more than a mortal, ingenious piece of physical clothing that we use in order to experience the physical world and that our personality, having departed the body, can travel through physical matter without any effort at all. That our physical garment can even be shared by other bodiless personalities; that we can leave it and return to it, and that bodiless personalities can even attempt to take it off you. Interesting! And, as we all know, like any garment, it will eventually wear out.

EVENT 8

The Box of Photos

Escaping Melbourne's inclement weather, I had moved north to tropical Queensland where I had been living for some years. It was a Saturday and like most days in the tropics, I woke to another typically perfect day. This particular Saturday was filled with great anticipation, as I was about to head off to the majestic Great Barrier Reef for my first-ever scuba dive with a friend.

We were blessed with calm seas and sunshine and the conditions could not have been better. We were soon on board the vessel and gently gliding through pristine turquoise waters. How invigorating it was to inhale that fresh salty sea air whilst we sat with our legs dangling over the edge of the bow, watching the glistening diamonds dance upon the vast ocean's surface.

We had enjoyed a wonderful and timeless few hours as we sailed towards our diving destination. Our relaxed conversation had been interrupted by the slowing of the boat. We had arrived. The crew jumped into action and we observed the animated scene with great enthusiasm for what was to come. Once the vessel had anchored and everything had been prepared, we excitedly geared up with our personally hired dive guide who was to take us down into the sensually warm tropical waters below.

It was everything that we had anticipated and more.

Together we swam over open, giant, iridescently striped clams the size of my body that clammed shut the moment that you cast a shadow over them. Colourful and curious fish of all shapes and sizes would envelop us and there were many amazing creatures to be found hiding among the great variety of corals that made up the magnificent underwater garden.

The time to resurface had come. We climbed back on board, and with a connecting glance we appreciated that we shared a special time together.

It was now lunchtime, and hungry from our activities, we enjoyed a long, drawn out smorgasbord fit for royalty.

With all wants and needs met, we gathered our towels to enjoy a stint of basking in the sun on the warm wooden deck. We passed the time in a mutual state of quiet ecstasy, lying side by side, his arm over mine, feeling the sun's rays on our bodies, enjoying our time together. It certainly had been a most perfect morning.

So here I was, feeling full of love for the sun, love for the sea, love for the diamonds dancing on the water, love for the world below with all of its magnificent creatures, love for my friend, love for my life experience – just love for love itself. It was a wonderful feeling, and I was enveloped in earthly bliss.

Then suddenly, around 1 p.m, ... *Voom!* Flashback!

Somehow out of the peace in my mind I was confronted with a picture of a previous "soul mate" being flashed in front of me. I hadn't seen this person for about a decade, nor had he been a part of my life for all that time.

Voom! Another flashback!

Voom! Another flashback!

Voom! Another flashback!

Voom! Another flashback!

Voom! Voom! Voom! Voom! Voom! One image after another kept flashing in front of me.

Memory after memory poured into my mind. Here I was in ecstasy with my new friend, whilst my mind was completely taken over by memories of a past partner!

This definitely didn't fit in with my present situation and was incredibly inconvenient. It didn't make sense at all.

As I continued to sunbathe, the flood of memories ran non-stop like a slide show.

As much as I wanted to give my full attention to being with my friend and staying in the lovely space that we had created, I couldn't, and as the memories kept flooding in, I became more and more emotionally affected and overcome by the sadness that I had felt all those years ago when my ex-partner and I had gone our separate ways.

Whilst lying on the deck, in between the memories flooding in, I tried to understand why this was happening, but no matter how hard I tried to find a link, it just didn't make sense. There was nothing that I could see in my 'new' friend that even remotely reminded me of my past partner. They certainly didn't look anything like each other and had lived very different lives along with very different backgrounds. Even their mannerisms were different. No matter how hard I tried to find a reason for what was occurring, I couldn't.

As pictures of my past relationship continued to bombard my mind, I thought about the past and why we had gone our separate ways.

We had separated through external circumstances not of our making, and even though our friendship remained, we went on separate journeys. It took many years for us to come to terms with our parting. Eventually he married a lovely lady, had two sons and a good family life.

I had enjoyed an incredibly deep bond with both him and his mother, which had been formed whilst the three of us lived together under the same roof. Although I was welcomed to be a part of their lives, I had chosen to stay away so that they could be free to create their own new lives together.

It had now been approximately ten years since our last contact, so having all these flashbacks on this special outing with my new friend really didn't make any sense at all. After about an hour of these flashbacks, tears began rolling down my cheeks, and my mood had changed from ecstasy to great sadness. I felt distraught.

How on earth was I going to explain this to my new friend? This whole situation was totally irrational. What was my new friend going to think of me? This was an incredibly awkward situation. I did my best to hide my feelings and cover any teary evidence so as not to spoil what had so far been a fantastic day.

"Are you OK?" my new friend asked, stroking my arm.

I was horrified. My tears had been discovered, and I was definitely not OK.

There was nothing else to do but share what was happening. To my great relief, my companion was indeed a true friend. He listened carefully without any interruption to what I was experiencing and gently wiped my tears as they continued to roll down my face.

The flashbacks and my tears flowed continuously throughout the remaining hours of the afternoon, both on board the boat as well as during the one-hour drive home. The dinner outing that we had planned for that evening had to be cancelled, as I was too emotional to go anywhere. My new friend lovingly stroked my hair until I eventually fell into a very deep sleep.

Ring-ring … ring-ring … ring-ring … ring-ring …

I was wakened by the sound of the telephone ringing. I glanced at the clock – 7.30 the next morning. *Who on earth calls anyone at 7.30 on a Sunday morning?* I asked myself, bounding out of bed and answering the phone. "Viviana speaking."

"G'day, Dean here."

I nearly fainted! It was my ex-partner in Victoria, the one I hadn't spoken with for ten years and whose memories had hijacked my outing to the reef the previous day.

He continued, "Do you remember the box of photos that I sent you when you were living in Amsterdam that got lost somewhere along the way and never arrived?"

How could I forget? I had asked Dean to send them over to me. They had never arrived and were apparently "lost at sea" somewhere in the process. We both loved art and photography, and many of the photos had been developed by us from film. Whenever we would go bush or camp out, the cameras came too. We had accumulated many great shots over our time together, and I was devastated that the box of photos had gone missing.

"Yes, I remember."

"Well I got a phone call from the local post office yesterday morning. They were renovating the premises, and they came across a box that had been placed high on a shelf and has been sitting there the whole time."

"Oh wow!" As I listened, the flood of memories during the previous day started to make sense as he continued to explain;

"My phone number was on the box, so they rang me to ask if I had ever lost a parcel headed to Amsterdam," he continued. "I knew immediately that it had to be the box of photos that we lost all those years ago, so I went over straight away and picked it up."

Dean went on to explain, "I got home around lunchtime and spent the whole afternoon going through all the photos."

I finally had a logical answer. I was at least now able to understand what had caused the memories to take over my mind during that previous afternoon!

Dean and I had had an amazing connection and experienced telepathy many times before, so I was not at all surprised that whilst he was sifting through the photos and memories on the previous day, I was receiving the images in my mind thousands of kilometres away.

I could only conclude at this stage that Dean's and my own wave frequencies were both finely tuned and very similar and that it wouldn't take much for our frequencies to share information being carried along them, no matter how far the distance.

I have experienced this on numerous occasions and come to understand that whether we are aware of this or not, our thoughts travel beyond ourselves and can unknowingly affect others. We are transmitters and receivers. Even from one side of the planet to the other. Distance is irrelevant.

EVENT 9

Acknowledgment of a Future Time

A COUSIN VISITING FROM HOLLAND had only ten days left before his departure to return home. I wanted to make sure that those ten days were going to be special, so I asked him, "Is there anything in Australia that you would like to see that you haven't seen?"

He responded speedily with "Uluru" – the site formerly known as Ayers Rock.

We were in Victoria, and if we allowed four days to drive to Uluru and another four to drive back, we could spend two days exploring Uluru and Kata Tjuta.

So we piled into the VW Kombi, and off we went.

A few days and some thousands of kilometres later, we arrived at the resort town of Yulara and headed to the supermarket for supplies.

The shopping centre square was centred around an open space meeting place and housed a supermarket, post office, information centre, news agency, take-away food shop, restaurant, gift shop, and an RM Williams clothing store.

As soon as I placed my foot down in front of the first shop, RM Williams, I was overtaken by a very strong, matter-of-fact acknowledgement. It was so business like that it shocked me and took me completely by surprise.

I'm going to be working here one day had flashed adamantly through my mind.

Where on earth did that thought come from? I was stunned. It wasn't as if I was overcome with the beauty of the shopping centre or had any desire or a dream or even a wish to live in the sweltering heat of the desert.

What a weird thought. I wasn't the slightest bit interested in working here. I shook the thought off immediately, giving it no more attention.

Although this statement had only stayed in my mind for a few seconds, I was completely thrown off guard by its almost dogmatic matter-of-factness, as if I seemed to have been given no free choice in the matter. It was rather strange.

With supplies purchased, we set up camp, visited Uluru and Kata Tjuta, and after a couple of days headed back to Victoria where I continued to live and work for some years.

I had been in a wonderful but somewhat demanding job for a few years, and although I had achieved great things, I couldn't see it expanding any further. It was time to do something different. The job had carried lots of responsibility, and I needed a change. I longed for something low-profile without any stress attached to give myself a break.

A friend recommended a company that placed people in the homes of elderly citizens needing assistance, and it sounded just perfect. I rang immediately and was appointed for a six-week period looking after a wonderful, frail lady of ninety years of age suffering dementia. I lived with her in her Melbourne home for four days per week, and I loved looking after her so much that six weeks became seven months, until she lost her ability to walk, and her family placed her in a nursing home.

The same company offered me another job, and I accepted. I had gone from living with a wonderful, gentle, petite lady, to now caring for a very large, grumpy old man.

I had only worked for three days in my new position and was already relieved that it was the first of my four days off. I headed down to a Brunswick Street Café.

I ordered my coffee, sat down and shortly afterwards the young lady with a strong accent came over with my cappuccino.

Recognising her accent, "You're Polish," I said with a smile.

She replied, "Yes, how did you know?"

"I have a very good friend who is Polish," I replied. "So how long have you been here?"

"I have been here for nearly a year, and I have to leave to go back to Poland in six weeks' time," she replied.

"What have you seen of Australia in your time here?"

"Nothing at all! I wanted to buy a van and travel around Australia, but it is so big and expensive that in the end I got a job and worked instead!"

I immediately liked her. She went on to explain that she was a medical student at university and deferred for a year to travel and see Australia. I felt sad that she had come all this way and hadn't been able to fulfil her dream.

"I have a motorhome," I shared with her.

Her excitement was impossible to miss. Her eyes lit up, and her voice elevated at least an octave higher.

"If I pay you five hundred dollars per week for the next six weeks would you take me around the west coast of Australia?" She could hardly blurt her words out fast enough.

I prepared the vehicle for the long drive. Anika hopped in, and off we drove.

It couldn't have been more perfect! I had also been wishing to explore the west coast as it was the only part of Australia that I had not yet seen. We were great company, and we both loved nature and bushwalking.

Anika was young and had obtained her driving license and let me know on several occasions that she could drive if I wanted to relax. Remembering how, when I first got my driving license, I was aching to get behind that steering wheel, I suspected that

Anika was going through a similar thing, so when we got to the beginning of the long straight road that cuts through the Nullarbor Plain, I handed her the keys and didn't get to see them again until the end of our trip. We had a ball!

I took thousands of photos and copied them all onto discs for Anika to take back to Poland so that she could revisit and share her amazing Australian journey with her family in Poland.

Anika had done lots of research before coming to Australia and knew exactly where she wanted to go and what she wanted to see. She took me to fascinating places that I never knew existed, and in turn, I had given her the means to get there. It was a tremendous partnership.

We went all the way along the west coast up to Darwin and continued down to Alice Springs where Anika was due to catch the train to Adelaide and fly from there back to Poland.

She had kept her word and paid five hundred dollars each week, which covered the cost of food and petrol, but she was now at the end of her savings. We had arrived in Alice with little money left but had had the time of our lives with a few days still to spare. I decided that I couldn't let Anika return to Europe without at least seeing Uluru, the "heart of Australia", and with my insistence, as my treat, off we went.

We had a fabulous time driving through the spectacular red dunes of the Simpson desert, with its sparsely dotted endless contrasts of spikey yellow spinifex-grass mounds. Having driven through many hours of melting heat, we finally arrived and as I had done the three-hour walk around "The Rock" before, I dropped Anika off at Uluru whilst I went to the supermarket in the nearby resort town of Yulara to pick up some food supplies before they closed.

Travelling with Anika had been great fun, and our journey together was now coming to an end. In a few days' time I would drop her off at the train station in Alice Springs, and I had no idea what I was going to do after that.

I parked in the car park behind the shops and walked into the small shopping centre. The first thing that I saw in my vision was a sign on a notice board straight ahead just inside the entrance. It read: "Gallery assistant required for Mulgara Art Gallery". Well! How lucky could one be! I had previously owned my own art gallery in Melbourne and had studied art at college. Needless to say, I got the job and started straight after I saw Anika off on the train in Alice a few days later.

It was a beautiful gallery housed in the foyer of the Sails in the Desert Hotel, just a ten-minute walk from the small shopping centre.

I worked there for nearly a year. The average stay for anyone working at the resort was three months, so I was considered one of the long-term residents.

I began to get a little bored in the gallery, but over the time that I lived there, I had fallen in love with the initially unwelcoming hot dry desert landscape and the experience of walking on that warm, soft red sand. I loved the peace, tranquillity and endless amount of space that the desert offered, and I loved walking the trails around Kata Tjuta and Uluru.

I went to the post office and caught a glimpse of a job advertised for the gift shop in the small shopping centre, I applied for the position and was appointed for the task. It was very similar to the gallery, and my yearning to do something different had not been satisfied.

A few months later, I learned that the shop just two doors away, was looking for a retail assistant, and I took the opportunity to fill the position.

So there I was, working behind the counter of my new job of just two weeks, when I look up from the counter, through the front glass pane to the outside footpath and all of a sudden I had a flashback: *I'm going to be working here one day!*

Wow. All those years ago, outside this very shop: RM Williams!

Until this moment I had completely forgotten about that.

How can that happen? How could I have been bombarded with the thought, all those many years ago, that I would be working in this very shop? It had been an acknowledgment of an already existing fact about a future time.

I remembered back to my car accident in my early twenties when I had a similar matter-of-fact acknowledgement: *I didn't think that I was going to die today.*

In that event I also knew without any doubt whatsoever that I had been given a pre-set date to die and that the day of the car accident was definitely the wrong day.

How very interesting!

I also remembered the film clip of my life, as if my whole life had been recorded and had flashed before my eyes just prior to my leaving my body.

This really got the neurons in my brain firing to figure out how this was at all possible. New questions invaded my mind:

Is everything in our lives pre-set?

Do we really have freedom of choice?

Are we living out some kind of pre-set program?

If wave frequencies can carry information, can it also carry the events of a pre-set program of our lives? Our journey?

Experiencing that we have future memory, just like we have a past memory, means our past, present, and future already somehow exists and if that is the case, can only mean that time itself, must actually be an illusion. Time had to be questioned.

Oh my God! I am feeling way out of my depth here! Who can I talk to! Who?

Life continued to throw me information that just didn't fit in with normal everyday life. How does this all fit together? I had experienced enough to know that life presented to be far more extraordinary than what it is generally believed to be and my intellect remained dedicated to seeking the truth behind our existence.

EVENT 10

The Buttoned-Up Jacket

I HAVE ALWAYS TAKEN GREAT delight in the art of dressing, with people often complimenting me on my dress sense. So it was a great surprise when a newly appointed supervisor requested my presence in her office and began with "The reason that I have asked you to attend this meeting is to inform you that your attire does not fit the company dress code. Therefore I am officially requesting that in future you dress in corporate attire, which is a buttoned-up jacket, skirt, stockings, and high-heeled shoes."

Well, I nearly fell off my chair!

I had been employed in the position for two years and seen many supervisors come and go, and none of them had ever pulled me up before. If ever I was called to an office it was usually to be either thanked or promoted.

I explained that due to an operation on my feet, high-heeled shoes were not a possibility. Having had both feet restructured and "flattened" due to overly high arches, I was physically unable to wear heels.

After some discussion, my supervisor relaxed her authority and we were able to come to a compromise. We decidedly agreed that I could wear long pants and low, comfortable shoes, but I would definitely have to adopt a buttoned-up jacket.

We were both happy with the compromise, and I was given a week to buy suitable attire.

My wardrobe was extensive, but purposefully void of anything that resembled a buttoned up jacket. I had always found them rather restrictive, incredibly uncomfortable and more in line with a strait-jacket to stop you waving your arms around in case you hurt yourself. I loathed ironing, and sending clothes to a dry-cleaner was a chore and expense that I preferred not to invite into my already busy and financially stretched lifestyle.

Where on earth could I possibly buy a jacket that I could cope with, let alone like? and the wave of thoughts kept coming;

I would really like a jacket that I wouldn't have to iron.
I want a jacket that I can throw into the washing machine.
I would love a jacket that is as comfortable as a windcheater.
I would really like a jacket that is colourful with a bit of flair.
A soft, woven, tweed woollen jacket that feels like a jumper.
A jacket that breathes and is made up from natural fibre.
Something different that suits my artistic lean.

By the end of the week I had a very clear idea of what I wanted whilst keeping in mind the criteria of a buttoned-up jacket.

Familiar with the city fashion stores I knew of no store where I was going to find a jacket that I would want to wear, at least not one that I could afford.

It was time for my ritual Saturday morning visit to Queen Victoria Market as I housed some delightful homestay students who needed to be catered for. I hopped in the car and headed off to gather fresh supplies.

As I drove towards the market, something very unusual happened. Without my intention, as I needed to drive straight ahead, my right arm rose and depressed the blinker lever, causing me to signal a right turn. My arms then turned the steering wheel, and I found myself doing a U-turn and heading away from the market.

Wow! This is really weird. What just turned my car around? Why am I driving in the opposite direction? Did I subconsciously do that, or did something else do that?

The blinker and U-turn were *not* on my agenda, and I felt "led".

As it was Saturday morning, the traffic was heavy, and in a state of confusion, I now found myself being carried with the flow of traffic in the wrong direction. It wasn't long before I was in the vicinity of a favourite place I would often frequent.

Having bought an old neglected house that I was in the process of renovating, I often called in to a second-hand furniture warehouse in a nearby suburb where I could buy cheap things to use for building material. I decided that whilst I was now heading in that direction, I might as well go and check it out.

I parked the car and entered the building. Heading straight to the used furniture section at the rear, I had to pass through a small Op shop at the front of the building to get there. I was about to go through the double door opening to the rear furniture section when I stopped in my tracks at the sight of a brand-new, stunning, stylish, and gorgeously colourful buttoned-up jacket, not hanging on a clothes rack like all the other clothes but displayed by itself. It was on a clothes hanger, hanging from a nail on the door frame leading into the rear furniture section.

It might as well have been thrown at me. What an odd place to hang a jacket! Had it not been hung in that odd place, I would never have seen it.

I couldn't believe my eyes. I had never seen such a beautiful jacket in my entire life. I fell instantly in love. It was in my hands before I could even think about grabbing it. The designer label was still hanging from the sleeve. It was by one of my favourite well-known designers. This was a brand-new jacket that I would not normally have been able to afford on my budget.

It was also a piece of contemporary artwork fashioned into a jacket, with an Andy Warhol design of Marilyn Monroe in bright colours, woven into a soft, woollen tweed fabric. It was beautifully edged in black trim and closed with shiny black beadlike buttons. It hugged the waistline with a wide black comfy windcheater-style stretch band, giving the impression of a wide belt. It had the same black stretch ribbed knit material as cuffs on the sleeves just like the cuffs on a windcheater!

Wow! Whether it would pass at work didn't even enter the equation. I had fallen in love with it, and I just had to have it.

I headed for the dressing room, praying that it would fit me. It was an unbelievably perfect fit.

This brand-new jacket would have normally cost hundreds, and I paid all of ten dollars. I was ecstatic! How incredibly fortunate I felt. I couldn't wait to wear it so I immediately went home, changed my clothes to suit, put on my new gorgeous jacket, and ecstatically headed off to the market as originally planned.

I wore that jacket every day for two weeks! I loved it so much that I couldn't get myself to wear anything else. This wasn't normally the way I utilized my clothing. Normally I would wear an article of clothing once or twice and then throw it in the washing machine.

I wore it all weekend. I wore it to work every day for two weeks straight (and surprisingly was not pulled up for it not conforming to corporate style). Two Saturdays later I woke up, thinking, *what am I going to wear today? I can't possibly wear my jacket again*, feeling a trifle disappointed.

Although the jacket was of natural fibre and breathed well, and I changed the clothing underneath it, it really was time to throw it in the washing machine!

I looked into my wardrobe for something different to wear but I just didn't want to wear anything else. I started thinking, *what I really need is another jacket, exactly the same, so that I could wear one and wash the other.* Then I had an even better thought: *No, what I really need is another jacket exactly the same, but in different colours, so that people wouldn't think that I never washed my clothes!*

A little embarrassed, I thought, *If I keep my arms close to my body, I could get away with wearing it just one more day.*

Well! *How disgusting was that?* I thought, as I put it on again. With all that Dutch blood running through my veins, I was known for my almost obsessive cleanliness, and this really wasn't like me at all.

As with all Saturday mornings, it was another routine market day, and so I headed off to Queen Victoria Market in my now slightly smelly, worn every day for two weeks, gorgeous jacket. Then:

I don't believe it!

I just don't believe it!

Oh my God! I don't believe it!

My right arm rose to push the blinker lever, and both my arms turn the steering wheel into a U-turn just as they did two weeks earlier, as if I was guided again to make the turn.

I was again driving in the wrong direction!

Unlike last time, when I was in a state of confusion, I am now, instead, incredibly excited to say the least: *Oh my God! Am I getting another jacket?* I was gushing with anticipation. *I must be getting another jacket! Oh my God! I'm getting another jacket!*

There was no need to question as to where I was going and the hardest thing now was to stay within the speed limit.

Like a little girl who was just about to be given free time in a candy store, I couldn't wait to get there! I had come alive with delight and total expectation. *Oh my God, Wow! I'm getting another jacket! Just like before! Wow!*

I parked the car and bolted into the op shop to get my other jacket!

I flew directly to the spot where I had seen the first jacket, and I was in total shock to see that there was no jacket.

It just didn't make sense at all.

Struck with incredible disappointment and disbelief, I look around the walls in dismay and still, no jacket. I frantically sifted through rack after rack like a wild woman hunting, until all racks were completely ransacked, and still no jacket.

The questioning process began:

Why did my car do what it did just like last time and not give me a jacket this time? Something made me turn my vehicle around two weeks ago and I end up with my jacket so why on earth did something turn me around this time and there's no jacket? I don't get it; it doesn't make any sense.

Was I meant to go somewhere else?

Did I miss what I was supposed to do?

Where else in this area should I have gone?

What made me turn around in the first place?

I was totally baffled. It was all too weird for me to figure out, and I was left disappointed and terribly disillusioned. I decided to leave the world of the can't-explain and get back to the world that could be explained. I sadly exited the shop and had one foot on the footpath when – "Excuse me" – a small voice cut through the air.

I hesitated. Was this woman calling out to me? I turned around to check.

I almost fainted.

There stood a woman staring straight at me, holding up a clothes hanger on which was hung the identical jacket, brand-new designer label still hanging off the sleeve, obviously the same size, but just a different colour!

There are simply no words to describe how I felt at that moment when I saw what I was looking at. I was overcome by so many different feelings, gushing through me with a million questions, that I haven't the slightest hope of being able to describe it.

Needless to say, I was left wondering: *How does this fit in to daily life?*

I was now in my forties, and this experience brought up the memory of the involuntary sharing of my body with an invisible aboriginal boy running over the rocks at Wilson's Promontory National Park when I was in my young teens.

It also brought me back to the memory of being squashed against the wall by something invisible in the house that I had rented in my college days, causing the cat, my flatmate, and myself all to flee in fear.

I have experienced many times that our physical bodies can certainly be guided.

The questions remained; who or what assisted me in turning my car around? How was it that both of those jackets were presented to me in such an obvious way?

Those jackets were perfect, and I could not imagine better jackets to suit. They met all my desires of what I both needed and wanted, not to mention getting two of them in different colours as I had wished for.

Are we, as humans, able to manifest what we want?

At this stage of my life I contemplated whether we are completely in charge of what we can manifest, or if we can manifest at all. For if that is so, why haven't I won the lottery yet? Believe me, I have seriously tried!

My experiences still leaving me to ponder the existence of another dimension beyond our awareness from which our lives are influenced. How else can I explain my car turning around twice and the receiving of both jackets on those two occasions? For now, I had to leave these pieces of the great jigsaw puzzle on the pile with all the other pieces still waiting to find their place.

EVENT 11

A Surprise Visitor
in My Gallery

I HAD RENTED THE FIRST floor of a building in a busy street not far from the central business district in Melbourne. It consisted of one massive room with wooden floorboards and a series of arches along the walls.

The space was filled with natural light streaming in through a stunning, ornate window overlooking the street. It had great potential to be an art gallery but was in need of much work.

After months of hard work and finding art to hang on the walls from various artists, I was ready to open the gallery.

I just loved the gallery and was proud of what I had accomplished. I often thought, *If only my father were still alive and could have seen this. I'm sure that he would have been proud of what I have achieved!*

I still had a full-time job in the city. I opened the gallery from 6 p.m. until 10 weekdays and all day Saturday and Sunday to see how the gallery fared and if it could eventually support me.

I loved being in the gallery so much that on some nights I would lock up at 10.00 p.m. and, instead of going home, would put on some great dance music and dance around the gallery, having the time of my life. Such joy!

One night after closing, whilst I was dancing to my heart's content, another unusual event shook my world.

My body had started to make strange, abrupt, jerking movements in my wrists, arms and shoulders. My hands began to twitch. My first thought was that I was having some kind of fit, even though I didn't suffer from epilepsy or anything like that.

I was completely out of control of my body, and this was not a *normal* situation at all!

I was really concerned about my welfare. The fact that I was unable to control my movements was frightening. I was jerking around all over the place. A very uncomfortable feeling came over me until suddenly I realised that there was rhythm to these jerky movements and that I somehow knew them – they were familiar.

With a mix of fear and intrigue, I naturally began the questioning process that always consumes me when unexplainable events take over:

What is happening to my body?
This is familiar.
Where do I know this from?
This is not a fit.

Still bopping around uncontrollably and confused at recognizing that I somehow knew these movements, I suddenly realized that I was not having a fit but rather that my body was actually dancing in a rhythm and style that was definitely not my own.

The more my body moved in this way, the more familiar it seemed. I felt terribly uncomfortable during the abrupt staccato movements, and I wanted them to stop.

The moment I wanted the unbidden movement to stop, my body stopped jerking about, and I regained control.

Feeling somewhat perturbed, I walked to my desk, sat down, and proceeded to process what had just happened.

I suddenly recognized the all-too-familiar staccato dance style. It even made sense, and it didn't surprise me once I recognized it. My father was both a gifted dancer and a talented artist. Both my parents were great dancers, and I remembered attending a family Dutch ball when I was still very young.

The large hall was full of people. My parents and approximately twenty other couples got up on the dance floor to do a tango. It was one of the most magnificent dance sequences that, to this day, I have ever witnessed (and having been a dance teacher myself, I have witnessed a few). I was in awe of my parents as my father began abruptly throwing my mother around the floor as she kicked and threw back her head. The dance had barely started when, one by one, the other couples ceased to dance, moving to the side and handing the floor over to my parents. I stood amazed amongst the onlookers. Everyone stood in awe, captivated, watching from the edge of the dance floor until they had finished, and the hall resounded with applause.

My father had a unique staccato style all his own. Growing up with my father I witnessed his constant clicking and snapping of his fingers with his own unique staccato wrist movements that constantly ruled our lives. *Oh my God!* I recognized without a doubt. *It's Dad's unique Latin staccato dance style! How could my own deceased father be able to control my body like that, and why?*

My father was both an artist and a dancer, and here I was, dancing in my own beautiful art gallery. Why *wouldn't he* want to join me in my celebration?

So once again I was shown that there are deceased, invisible personalities who are still very much alive and in some cases even have the capability of joining us in our bodies, even though only for a brief moment in time.

In my early teens, running over rocks, I was joined and carried by the invisible personality of an aboriginal boy.

In my twenties I was left gasping for air when I was squashed by an invisible presence against a wall.

In my forties, my arms strangely make a U-turn, twice within a fortnight.

And now still into my forties, my deceased father jumps into my body and takes over to physically dance and celebrate with me.

Needless to say then, for me, by now, there is no doubt whatsoever that we have a personality that continues to live beyond physical death and that it is still very much alive, long after our physical bodies are deceased.

That much I have been shown, but many pieces still need to be understood.

EVENT 12

I Know Everyone Intimately

ONE OF MY MOST unusual and, in many ways, liberating moments in this life was when one Saturday morning I went to the Queen Victoria Market to do my usual weekly food shopping.

It was a stunning, sunny day, reflecting a brilliant blue sky with not a cloud in sight. We still had plenty of supplies, so rather than take the car, I decided to walk with the small shopping trolley instead.

As always, I had a great time shopping at the market amidst all the hustle and bustle, and I delighted in being surrounded by so many different personalities all busily doing their thing.

After my shopping, I stopped to enjoy a band from Peru playing beautiful, haunting sounds on wooden flutes of the Andes, which seemed to resonate through the core of my being.

I remember feeling peaceful and happy – and blessed just to be there and enjoy the many colourful experiences that life offered.

It was one of the happiest times in my life. I was renovating my first house, and I was also looking after some absolutely delightful overseas homestay students who were having one of the greatest times in their own lives. We were a happy bunch, sharing wonderful times together, with lots of fun, laughter and creativity.

With my shopping completed and a trolley full of fresh foods I waded through the market towards home. As I commenced the uphill stroll with my shopping bags and trolley in tow, I had a strong urge to stop and look back towards the market, now some fifty metres away. So for no reason other than to follow an urge, I did just that. I turned around and looked down at all the people hurrying and scurrying about.

People of many different nationalities were rushing about, carrying bags, bartering for goods, hurriedly weaving across the roads through the constant flow of traffic. It was a real buzz to take all this in visually, and at the same time, I felt as if I was in a vacuum of peace, when all of a sudden I got a massive shock.

It didn't matter who I looked at or what nationality they were, I *knew,* without any doubt whatsoever, every single person *intimately.*

Intimately! Oh wow!

How was that possible?

It was an awesome experience standing there looking into the crowd of thousands, knowing that somehow I knew every single person that my eyes fell upon.

I recognized every single person I looked at as someone that I had known intimately before.

I can't even begin to explain what that felt like.

As usual, the questions flew into my mind.

But how could I possibly know all these people?

Where could I possibly know them from?

When did I ever spend time with them?

How could I possibly have spent time with all of those people?

This was another one of those "This doesn't compute" events, and I again found myself thinking of how inadequate my schooling for all those years had been. I was never taught about anything like this; I was lost for an explanation.

I so wished that I had someone to turn to for answers! It was frustrating that none of these types of events ever seemed to happen to people around me. I often wondered about my own existence. Did I get lost and end up on the wrong planet?

Some months later, I had another such experience.

It was peak hour, and traffic was heavy. I had just walked to the other side of a major intersection in the Melbourne business district and stood on the footpath on the corner of Elizabeth and Collins Streets. For a moment I became overwhelmed by all the noise of the trams, buses, and cars and the thousands of people rushing to catch them. Feeling claustrophobic, I needed some space, so I stopped next to a pole in the midst of all the chaos and looked up at the infinite blue sky above me. A sense of peace relaxed me as I stood staring into space. After a few minutes I lowered my head and looked into the rushing crowd – and *Wow!*

It was just like what had happened at the Queen Victoria Market.

No matter who I looked at, I *knew* every single person intimately. Every single person! It was a strange realisation and one that was at the time, hard to grasp. There were thousands of people, and I knew them all. I knew each person as well as you would know a close family member or a close friend or partner.

No matter who I looked at, I had known every person in a close and intimate way.

These two experiences have certainly left me in awe of this amazing life. We are far more than we dare to think. There is so much more going on in this life than we know about, than what we can physically see or hear, which we have yet to fully understand or even discover.

So now, in my forties, from all these experiences so far and a great many others, I felt confident that we are all somehow intimately and deeply intertwined and connected to each other, regardless of culture or any other superficial differences.

I can best describe it in this way:

Imagine sailing through the ocean, and as the boat ploughs through the water, individual droplets of water splash up. For a moment in time, the droplets of water travel as something separate from the ocean and eventually return to be part of the greater ocean once again.

These last two experiences made me feel that there is an aspect within each of us that comes from the same source. Like the droplets, and for a moment in time (which we call life), an aspect of ourselves has become separated as individuals from that source. And when the physical garment of our lives is spent, that particular aspect of our individual selves will reunite with our source and be together again as one phenomenon, just as the droplets return to the ocean.

I feel certain that there are many aspects involved in the making up of our human experience. With the experiences that I have had, I cannot dismiss the possibility of control or interference from another dimension beyond our awareness. I have no doubt that apart from our physical organic bodies, there are wavelengths, frequencies, personalities, and who knows how many other facets that all come together and each play an imperative role in our experience as human beings in order to create the magnificence of that which we are. Just as white light can be split into many colours, I believe that our human experience can also be split into many facets.

EVENT 13

Being Watched as I Move into My Apartment

A VAN FULL OF BELONGINGS was parked in the driveway. In the process of moving into my new abode, I wrapped my arms around my TV set, ready to take it inside.

I felt a piercing, almost laser-like sensation (hard to describe) enter my body through my back, travelling straight through to exit from my front directly in line with my television set. This was accompanied by a strong feeling that someone behind was watching.

I let go of the TV and immediately turned around to where the feeling was coming from. I homed in on a couple of upper-storey windows on a high-rise housing commission building in the distance. It felt as if someone in one of those windows was checking out the goods in my car through a telescope. The windows were too far away and too small for me to see into them, and after a good long stare in that direction, I turned back to my van and continued to unload, all the while with that strong sense that someone was watching my every move.

After I had finished moving into the apartment, I locked up and headed to my mother's place in the country for a few days.

The following day, Mum and I were playing a game of Scrabble when suddenly I *knew* that at that very moment someone had broken into my apartment, and I was being robbed.

I looked up at my Mum and said, "Oh my God, Mum! I'm being robbed!"

Typically, my mother ignored me as if she had some kind of selective hearing that instantly tuned out whenever one of these unexplained situations popped up. She wasn't interested, and as usual, I was frustrated.

"Mum! I'm being robbed! Right now! Someone is in my apartment robbing me right this very moment!"

Mum lifted her head to look at the Scrabble board with an indifferent "Yeah, yeah" and continued concentrating on her next brilliant word without commenting or even acknowledging what I had just expressed. She laid down a word and said, "Your turn."

This lack of acknowledgment about anything unexplainable was one of my greatest frustrations. I knew that it was futile to mention this again because my mother would only say something like "Oh you're just imagining things again."

I dropped it, and we continued playing Scrabble. After a lovely evening together, despite the fact that I knew that I'd been robbed, I made an early night of it in readiness for a lovely fresh start in the morning.

Breakfast in Mum's garden was always a pleasure, followed by some housework, and soon it was time for me to go home. We said our goodbyes, and off I drove, wondering what was in store.

I finally arrived at my new apartment to find that I had indeed been broken into and "cleaned out" of my TV, radio, CD player, and many other items.

I had already grasped that information was carried by wavelengths and frequencies and that we can transmit and receive, but what part of our anatomy are we receiving the information through? How are we able to decipher it? How could I know and feel the exact moment that my apartment was being broken into, when I was over one hundred and fifty kilometres away? And what purpose is there to this awareness? There were still many things to understand.

How could I have best dealt with that knowledge at the time?

With that question, a possible scenario played out in my mind:

Ring-ring … ring-ring ….

"Constable Johnny Bubble speaking."

"Hello, Constable Bubble, I was wondering if a policeman was available to rush over to my apartment, as I am being robbed as we speak."

"Are you in or near your apartment now?"

"No, I'm one hundred and fifty kilometres away."

"Well, how do you know that you are being robbed?"

"Because I just picked up the information through a wavelength" *Click!*

"Hello? Hello?" (Dial tone.) "Constable Bubble, are you there?"

Humans are capable of incredible sensitivity, sensing events occurring hundreds of kilometres away. We are all linked.

Analysing the two separate events where I knew every single person in a crowd of thousands intimately, and having already understood that we are transmitters and receivers, able to receive information such as "I am now at this very moment being robbed", I begin to question even more deeply.

We know that in the human brain, information is passed from one neuron to another without their having any physical contact. We scientifically know that there are chemical reactions and electrical charges jumping from one neuron to another.

The brain is also full of incredibly complex electrical and chemical systems.

I can only conclude that just like the neurons in our brain, we are passing information from one person to another but in a much larger brain called the cosmos, complete with its electrical storms/charges and vast array of chemistry.

EVENT 14

Blue Energy Rises
from My Body

I WAS INTO MY MENOPAUSAL time of life. My body seemed 'all over the place', and normal patterns had become increasingly irregular.

I had become anaemic. A blood test found that my red cell count was dangerously low, and if it dropped any lower, I would need a blood transfusion. I was already due to go into hospital the following week for an operation relating to this matter.

It was late afternoon, and Mum and I were both home relaxing. She was cooking soup in the kitchen, and I was resting in my room.

I got up to go to the bathroom, and on my way back to my room I collapsed into unconsciousness, gashing open my head on the corner of the concrete wall before falling to the floor.

I had completely blacked out and was lying flat on my back in the hallway. With my eyes still closed and still unconscious, I was looking down the front of my body as if seeing it with my eyes open (as if my chin was on my chest), looking down the length of the front of my body to my feet and beyond, into the hallway and my surroundings. I could see my mother sitting on the floor next to me, looking concerned, my right hand clasped in both of hers.

My head was still lying flat on the floor, and my eyes were closed, yet I was seeing everything.

Whilst my body lay in this unconscious state, I began to see a beautiful ethereal shape, deep turquoise in colour, rising very slowly out of my body. It was the same shape as the contour of

133

my physical body but wasn't solid, and I could see through it. The colour reminded me of the light blue part of a gas flame. It continued rising ever so slowly.

I suspected that my life was about to end and that my life force was departing my body. I witnessed the whole scene around me as clearly as if I were conscious, yet I was still totally unconscious on the floor. I had no fear and I was totally comfortable with what was happening to me.

My mother began to panic, and I could both see and hear her as she started hitting my hand, crying out my name over and over again. I also saw her vulnerability and her inability to cope with what was happening, and I felt great sadness for her as I heard her cry out, "Wake up, wake up! I don't know what to do! I don't know what to do!"

I had never seen my mother in such a vulnerable state before.

The blue ethereal duplicate shape of my body had now risen to perhaps one centimetre above my body, when I was overcome with great compassion for my mother. I couldn't leave her in that state, and the ethereal blue energy body lowered slowly back into my physical body.

I regained consciousness but was unable to open my eyes. With all my meagre strength, I managed to softly utter the words "It's OK, Mum; just help me up, and take me to my bed."

My mother helped me up but I only made it a couple of metres before I collapsed and fell flat on the floor, again lapsing into unconsciousness. Again I saw everything in front of me as if my eyes were open, and the blue ethereal energy began very slowly to rise out of my body again.

I understood that an essential part of my being alive was departing my body, and as before, I felt totally comfortable about that.

My mother was stricken with panic, and again I became deeply concerned for her well-being. Just as before, the blueness lowers slowly back into my body, and I regain consciousness.

With a lot of effort and still unable to open my eyes, I gently say, "It's OK, Mum. Just help me up, and get me to bed."

I was unable to open my eyes and relied on my mother's help to lead me.

This time we made it to the bed, and I fell heavily into it. My mother tucked me in, and I managed enough strength to softly say, "I'm OK, Mum, you can go now."

Mum left the room to attend the soup on the stove whilst in the meantime I lay in bed expecting to depart my body forever. I simply waited, at peace and ready to go.

The thought occurred to me, *What about Mum?* I needed to ease her mind to cope, so I harnessed all my remaining strength and called out, "Muuuuuummmmmm."

She entered my room, and with my left hand I tapped the bed as if to say, "Come and sit here," and she sat beside me on the bed. Still unable to open my eyes, I felt for her body and placed my hand on her thigh. I whispered, "I want you to know that you have done everything just fine, Mum. Everything is just right, thank you. You can go now."

Mum departed the room, and I was now lying in readiness to depart my life. I don't remember much after that, except that the blue energy didn't rise again.

I had split my head open when I first fell and had lost an amount of blood that I couldn't afford to lose because of my already low blood count. I went to hospital and had my operation along with two life-saving blood transfusions.

I feel blessed to have had this experience because it confirmed to me yet again that there is so much more to us than just the physical body.

Still in my forties and wondering just how many aspects were involved in the making up of a human being. I had to add my experience of an ethereal light body.

We really are rather amazing.

EVENT 15

Red Blood Cells

I WAS APPROXIMATELY FORTY-FIVE YEARS old when I heard about a meditation technique focusing on the interconnection between body and mind. It involved ten days of sitting in silence with up to twelve hours of disciplined meditation per day. The technique encouraged the self-exploration of the physical sensations of the body that continuously condition our state of mind. The purpose was to make it possible, through regular practice and increased awareness, to see how one's own thoughts, sensations, feelings, and judgements create one's experience.

Still searching for answers to many questions, I decided to enrol.

No eye contact or talking to other participants was allowed for the full ten days.

For the first three days we were taught to concentrate solely on the breath going in and out of our nose and to focus only on the area of the body below the nostrils and above the top lip. Any other bodily sensations that we might feel had to be totally ignored; for instance, if we had an itch, we were not to respond to it but instead continue to focus the mind only on the breath entering and exiting our body.

It really was the hardest physical thing I have ever done. Sitting on a cushion without moving the body at all, for twelve hours a day, with only a five minute break each hour (apart from food breaks), was painful agony. Trying not to be swayed by the mind was also definitely no easy task. In fact, it was so difficult that I even tried to get out of doing the rest of the course on only the second day.

Luckily for me, I wasn't the first to try to run away from all that uncomfortable sitting on a cushion, and they were able to persuade me to stick with it. After all, only very limited numbers of people were accepted for the retreat, and my being there meant that someone else had missed out. In addition, I had made a total commitment to finish the course when I enrolled.

So, successfully persuaded, I stayed on and faced another eight days of pain and discomfort on the cushion.

On the third day I was confronted by a totally new sensation. We had returned to the meditation hall after lunch break. The bell sounded to begin the next hour's session involving fifty-five minutes of sitting and a five-minute break. I sat down on my cushion, as still as a rock, focusing on my breath, eyes closed, and went into deep concentration.

I felt an amazing sensation of water pouring out through my nostrils. The sensation of water continued to envelop me, and it seemed to be everywhere. I started to feel embarrassed at the feeling that so much water was going to completely saturate me as well as the floor around me. I feared that I would be sitting in a puddle and that I had no idea how I was going to explain it.

As I had been instructed, although I was tempted to open my eyes, I ignored the sensation and continued to sit with my eyes closed and focus on the breath going in and out of my body.

The more I focused, the wetter I felt. It took a lot of discipline to keep my eyes closed and continue to endure the "water everywhere" sensation.

I dreaded the session coming to an end because I didn't know how I was going to be able to handle the wet floor around me or how I would react to what was happening. I sat with mixed feelings of concern, anxiety, confusion, and a great deal of curiosity. All the while sitting perfectly still, eyes closed, continuing to focus on my breath.

Finally, the fifty-five minutes passed, and the bell rang. It was the end of the sitting and the beginning of the five-minute break before another fifty-five minute session.

I was apprehensive about opening my eyes and looking at the floor and the puddle that I was sitting in. Courageously, I opened my eyes to face it.

I was totally surprised and amazed to find that I was perfectly dry.

I wiped my nose with the back of my hand, thinking that I would most likely catch some drips, but it too was perfectly dry.

Needless to say, I was relieved at this discovery, but what was all that water about? How could I have felt that so strongly and yet remain totally dry?

I was here to find answers, but instead, my list of questions grew. I reminded myself that this was only day three and that I had seven more days ahead to find my answers.

The first three days of learning to focus all of our attention on the nostril area of the body had come to an end, and the following morning we were instructed to go to the next stage of this method of meditation: sitting perfectly still with our eyes closed, but now taking all of our concentration through the various parts of the body in a sequence explained to us.

I had read somewhere that it was possible to see blockages in the body and unblock them using this method, so I was trying to look inside at the workings of my body. But all I could do was *imagine* travelling through my body. Hour after hour I spent the morning with eyes closed, seeing no more than what I would normally see if I just closed my eyelids. I wasn't "seeing" anything as I was going through this process. Many thoughts still invaded my mind:

What am I supposed to see here?
I can't see anything.
Am I doing this right?
What am I really doing here?
This is agony. I want to go home.
I can't believe that I am doing this to myself.
This is a total waste of time.
Stop thinking!
We're not supposed to think!
Concentrate!

No matter how hard I tried to stop thinking, the thoughts continued to invade my mind. I was really looking forward to breaking for lunch and stretching my body. Time seemed to drag on forever.

Donnnngggggggg.

Oh, what a relief to hear the sound of that bell ring!

Like Speedy Gonzalez, I couldn't get off that cushion fast enough. Phew! For now at least, it was a welcome escape from mental monotony and the torture of bodily discomfort.

I wanted so much to ask the other participants if anyone was experiencing anything, but the rules dictated there must be no eye contact or speaking throughout the retreat.

I had to bite my tongue very hard and strain my neck not to look up at anyone. It was a real lesson in self-control along with the rest of the course.

Donnnngggggggg.

Lunch was over all too soon when the bell sounded, calling us back to the hall for the afternoon sitting. I really wasn't too eager to return, and it was no accident that I was the last person to enter the hall and sit on the cushion.

With everyone now seated on their cushions and ready for the next sitting, the bell rang again for the beginning of the next fifty-five minute session.

I took my meditation position and closed my eyes.

Oh my God, what is that?

Unlike in the morning sessions when on closing my eyes I saw nothing but the back of my eyelids, this is a totally different experience;

My eyes are closed, and I'm sitting in meditation pose like a rock. I am looking straight ahead at brightly coloured, red froth.

What is that? What am I looking at?

The froth is just like the froth that you get when you whip up egg whites, only this is bright red, the colour of blood, and there is nothing to see anywhere in my vision except for this bright red froth.

Is this blood I am looking at? I almost can't believe what I am seeing, but there is no mistaking that what I am looking at is very real.

I am seeing this as clearly as you would see something that you were looking at with your eyes open, except that my eyes are closed.

The froth bubbles get bigger and bigger as I travel into and through the space between the bubbles.

As I pass through the space between the red bubbles, they get bigger and bigger as my capacity to see; my vision; becomes more and more microscopic. It is as if I have become smaller than a microscopic dot. Now, rather than something that visually resembles froth, I see large individual bubbles suspended in black space, passing me on all sides, and the bubbles continue to get bigger as I travel through this black space between them. I continue to become smaller and smaller, and I feel as minuscule as a pinprick travelling between these bubbles. They are now huge and becoming fewer in number.

Suddenly I find myself floating forwards between two now gigantic bubbles, and beyond them there are no more bubbles. (The last two bubbles are so big that it feels like being suspended between two high-rise buildings.)

I am now confronted with an infinite black void into which I am about to fall.

I am inside the experience of what I am seeing, and I have no doubt whatsoever that this experience is as real as the experience of sitting on the cushion – and as real as you reading these words right now.

Total panic engulfs me as I am about to fall into this endless black space, the black void, the nothingness of infinity in front of me.

A gasping sensation accompanies my fear.

My mind bursts into action, and my panic escalates.

If I go into that black space, I'll never find my way back!

The moment that fear sets in, my vision sweeps to the right, even though I remain unmoving and as still as a rock on my cushion.

I am now looking at a section of a huge rubbery-looking beige tube suspended in dark maroon coloured space. It looks big enough for me to stand up inside it.

My thoughts struggle to make sense of this experience:

What is this?

What am I looking at?

Am I seeing inside my own body?

Is this a vein?

What is that moving inside the tube?

A very faint luminescent glow behind the tube lets me see a faint silhouette travelling slowly through it. The shape is similar to a rubber dinghy and takes up nearly the whole width of the tube as it passes through at an angle, the bottom slightly ahead of the top.

I am totally amazed and full of intrigue and wonder. I am no longer frightened as no black void confronts me, and the falling sensation is gone. Instead, I have something to look at, and the experience feels like being inside and in the middle of an amazing organic environment.

What am I looking at here?

The questions rise up in my mind:

Is that a single blood cell travelling through a capillary?

Wow! What else could it be?

Oh my God! How is this possible?

How can I be seeing this without a microscope?

Donnnngggg. The bell sounded.

What? Already? I just sat down a couple of seconds ago!

I couldn't believe that the fifty-five minute session had come to an end. The whole experience had only taken a second in my own measure of time, as if I had barely sat down and closed my eyes! What happened to time?

Wow, what a sitting! What an incredible and amazing experience!

During our five-minute break, my mind tracked back immediately to a situation that had occurred many years before, whilst I attended a work conference at Griffith University in Brisbane.

I was sitting at a table enjoying a lunch break with other colleagues also attending the conference. The café was crowded, with little room between tables. Although I was trying to give my colleagues my full attention, I kept catching snippets of a conversation from the table directly behind me.

Whilst our table were discussing the conference, the table behind me were quietly discussing how human beings were able to see atoms and molecules without the need of a microscope.

The more snippets I caught, the more fascinated I became until eventually, I just had to excuse myself, turn around, and interrupt: "I'm really sorry but I couldn't help overhearing your conversation, and I am totally fascinated. I would so much like to join you and listen in. Would that be all right?"

The two men were happy for me to join them. Soon I was sitting at their table in the hope that I might finally get some answers.

I listened as one of the men shared an experience in which, through meditation, he could concentrate his vision to "shrink" far enough to "see" down to the molecular structure of things.

Even though I had already experienced a whole range of unexplainable events, I continually had to remind myself to keep an open mind as I listened. I was convinced that the man sharing his account of what he had experienced believed in what he had experienced and that he was telling "his truth".

I was totally fascinated, as I had only experienced events outside or external to my body. I had never had an "internal" experience.

It was great for me to have listened to this man because for once the situation had been reversed. I now fully understood the difficulty people had in accepting such unusual events when they themselves had never experienced events of that nature.

It was quite confronting for me to feel my response to his sharing and to have the "shoe on the other foot", so to speak.

I showed my respect to the person who had kindly shared his experience. I was grateful for the opportunity to listen, and all I could do with this information was keep an open mind, not judge it as either true or false, and accept that it was his experience.

And now here I was, years later, and through meditation able to "see" down to what appeared to be my own red blood cell level without the use of a microscope. To say I was excited was a huge understatement!

I couldn't wait to get back onto that cushion to see what else I might discover. The bell couldn't ring fast enough for me, and excitedly I went into the next fifty-five minute session.

To my great disappointment, there were no other extraordinary events during the remaining six days of the meditation retreat.

From this experience I had discovered that it was indeed possible for human beings to see the "internal" workings of their own physical bodies through silent, focused meditation.

I had also learnt that time differs in different situations.

How can fifty-five minutes also be a convincing one and a half seconds?

I recall questioning time itself after an earlier event at the swimming pool, when I left my body, and time continued whilst, all the while, in that bodiless state, I was looking down at the "frozen in time" scenario below. I saw how time had split into "time functioning" and "time frozen", two different time scenarios.

These were not the only events that had me questioning time itself, and I will cover more on the subject later in the book.

EVENT 16

A Foreigner on a Pushbike

J AY AND I CLICKED immediately.

After our meeting was over, he invited me out for lunch, and I happily accepted the invitation.

Over lunch he mentioned that his previous partner had recently been on a holiday and met someone else, so although they remained friends, they were no longer together.

I didn't ask questions as I detected a tone of sadness in his loss of her affections. I figured that he would tell me more when he was ready. We had a great deal in common and were able to share a healthy variety of topics. Our mutual attraction was strong, and I knew that it was highly likely that we would see each other again.

I was living in the country at this time and had been given the key and use of a friend's house in Melbourne during his absence overseas.

Having completed a task in South Gippsland, I headed off to Melbourne for the weekend. As usual when travelling on that particular road, I stopped at a picturesque seaside inlet to smell the clean sea air, listen to the squawking of seagulls and inject myself with a strong dose of coffee.

I pulled over by the café and heard on the radio that a terrible storm was heading straight towards us. Looking up at the sky I could see the heavy clouds in the distance rolling in. This was not your average storm and resembled a very dark, morbid monster coming in to swallow everything up. I was grateful that I was not heading south towards Wilsons Promontory as they were certainly in for a very wet, turbulent spell. I figured that I had just enough

151

time for my coffee before the approaching waterfall would pour down upon us.

I grabbed my takeaway coffee and walked to the shoreline to sit and enjoy what was left of the calm before the storm.

I noticed a man with a pushbike laden with belongings, sitting at a picnic table and contemplating the dark, incoming clouds. He was obviously a traveller. His clothes made me suspect that he was most likely European.

I found a nice place to sit and as I sipped my coffee, the sky grew darker, the seagulls disappeared, and I knew that the heavens above were about to break open.

Yes, I thought, *this is going to be a very nasty storm!*

I could now smell the rain in the air and wanted to get to my van before it started, so I quickly finished my coffee. The shortest way to the van was straight across the park, where I crossed paths with the man on the bike who was looking rather worried.

"Hello," I said as I passed him.

"Hello," he responded with a strong Swiss accent.

I felt sorry for him as I continued to walk to my van, and ten metres beyond him, I turned to enquire, "This is going to be a really nasty storm. Where are you off to?"

"I was to ride my bike to Wilsons Promontory Park, but I'm not sure if the storm will let me. It is not looking so good."

Wilsons Promontory was my favourite place on earth, and I knew the road well. By car it would take about two and a half hours.

"How long will it take you to ride there on your bike?" I asked.

"I thought maybe two or three days to arrive there," he replied.

I felt compassionate. This was not a good situation for him at all. He seemed like a lovely person, and I had travelled overseas a great deal myself and help was always given to me whenever I needed it, so I decided that it was now my turn to help a traveller in need.

"You could put your bike and belongings in the back of my van, and I would be more than happy to drive you to the camping ground at Wilsons Promontory if you so wish."

"I would be very grateful, but it is a long way, and a lot to offer. It is really a very long way," he replied.

"It's OK. Bring your bike, and let's get into the van before the rain pelts down." I began running to the van to make room for the bike.

We quickly prepared for the journey to the Prom, and no sooner had we hopped into the van than the rain pelted down like a thick grey blanket. It was going to be a very long, slow drive to the Prom in this weather! I looked over at my companion with a reassuring smile, and he looked incredibly relieved. I was glad that I had been able to take this man out of the awful predicament that had befallen him.

We drove for nearly three hours, and it was one of the worst storms that I had ever driven through. We talked throughout the whole journey, and I enjoyed listening to the many wonderful adventures that he had experienced whilst travelling by bicycle around Australia. He enjoyed listening to my experiences about chance meetings, coincidences, and synchronicities, such as that I had arrived at just the right time to catch him going to my favourite place, that I was a fellow traveller driving a van as opposed to a car allowing me to carry his bike, and that I just happened to be free and available to assist.

Synchronicity was one of my favourite topics. I had experienced a lot of remarkably unique moments of unbelievable synchronicity throughout my life, and it always fascinated me.

With all that chatting, the journey flew by quickly, and before we knew it, we drove into the Wilsons Promontory camping ground.

We found a campsite, set up camp for the night, drove to the café for dinner, and returned to our camp to retire for the night.

The Swiss man had pitched a tiny one-man tent in the pouring rain, and I found myself, once again, feeling sorry for him but my generosity didn't want to extend to sleeping with him on the single mattress in my little van. I did feel a bit mean though.

It was to be a long night of howling winds and bucketloads of rain for the poor foreigner. I hoped that he would be all right out there, exposed to the raging elements, whilst I guiltily cuddled my warm, dry doona, in my cosy little "cubby house" van, which was permanently set up for comfortable camping in any conditions.

As the morning dawned, I woke up wondering if the man on the bike had been either blown away by ferocious winds or drowned in the torrents of rain. I wound down my window and called out for a sign of life: "Hello, Mr. Switzerland, are you awake?"

He muttered something that I didn't quite understand and then said, "Ah, yes, I am awake."

"I will be heading back to Melbourne soon and I would like to invite you to share some breakfast at the café before I go. Would you care to join me?" I asked.

"Yes, I will come," he replied and off we drove, through the shallow lakes that had formed overnight, to the camp café.

Instead of a quick breakfast as I had intended, we chatted for a couple of hours until I finally decided that it was time for me to head back to Melbourne. It was time to say our goodbyes.

"Well, Mr. Switzerland, it was a pleasure, and I really enjoyed my detour, but I need to head off now. How long will you stay here at the Prom?" I asked.

"I don't really know," he answered.

"Well, this storm isn't going to pass quickly, and I think that it will be at least a few days, if not longer before it will clear up. Will you be all right?"

"Yes, I will stay here for at least one week. Thank you for the ride."

I wished him well, and as it was still raining heavily, left him at the café where he could at least stay dry. No contact details were exchanged, as it wasn't likely that our paths would ever cross again, and our lives continued on our separate journeys.

As I drove off through the camping ground I could see that there were no other campers and that he would probably only have the café staff and rangers to communicate with. Due to the inclement weather pattern of the Prom at this time of year, it was the quietest time, and the camping grounds were usually deserted.

I thought of how boring it might be for him to just be sitting in a characterless, cold, canteen-style café for a week, trying to stay dry.

I decided to call into a bookshop when I reached the nearby township of Leongatha and purchased a book that I had previously read about synchronicity. I'd had a lot of fun reading it and decided to send it to him so that he could at least have something interesting to read. I didn't know his name so I addressed it "To the Swiss man travelling by bicycle, c/o Tidal River Café" and sent it off without any return address or contact details, as I was sure that it would find him. A good deed done, I could now continue on with my own life.

I spent the weekend enjoying my time in Melbourne before returning home to the country and concentrated on my job and, naturally, Jay, who I hoped would get over his broken relationship soon so that I might see him sometime in the near future.

Two weeks later, I decided to spend another weekend in Melbourne and headed off down the princess highway to my friend's vacated property in North Melbourne.

The following morning I received a phone call: "Hi, it's Jay here. I thought I'd give you a call to see if you would like to catch up for coffee."

"Oh, hi, Jay. Yes, that would be lovely, but I'm in Melbourne right now, and I won't be back till Monday. But I would love to see you again."

"Whereabouts in Melbourne are you?"

"I'm in North Melbourne," I replied.

"What a coincidence! I'm in North Melbourne too! What are you doing for lunch today?"

For a moment I wondered if he was stalking me, as Melbourne was indeed a very large city, and here we both were in the same place yet both living two hours' drive away. I guessed that he might have rung my phone number in the country and spoken with my mother, who might have mentioned that I was in North Melbourne for the weekend. Either he may have decided to head there himself to try to catch up, or it was just another of those many amazing coincidences.

I left it at that and continued with the phone conversation. "Well, I haven't made any set plans, so we could catch up if you wish."

"That's great! Then let's have lunch together."

We set a time to meet, and I was looking forward to seeing him again.

Lunch was fabulous and I enjoyed his company immensely just as I had the first time we had lunch together. We talked through the hours of the afternoon, and the day passed quickly. He offered to cook me dinner, as he loved cooking. So we did some shopping, and as the evening was starting to eat away the day, he began to prepare a special meal. I was looking forward to discovering his culinary skills, as ironing and cooking were the two tasks in my life that I would do almost anything to get out of. I preferred the washing up to cooking every time.

He was a fabulous chef and could have run a classy restaurant, to say the least. I was impressed, and after our amazing dinner we moved into the lounge to relax with a glass of wine.

Jay stretched out along the couch and I plonked myself on the soft carpeted floor nearby with my back against a lounge chair.

After some chatting and a little wine, we relaxed into the evening, and Jay decided to share what had happened with his previous partner and what he was going through with that whole ordeal.

I was ready to listen and gave him the freedom to let it all out.

He began to tell me how a few months earlier his partner of many years had decided to go on a long journey, and after a couple of months, she met a man who would change their lives forever.

She had fallen in love with this new man, and although they had only a short time together, she couldn't get him out of her mind. This other man had made such an impression on her that she couldn't go back to her relationship with Jay, leaving him devastated and clinging to a sliver of hope that it would all blow over and that one day they might possibly reunite. He had been told that this new man had gone to Tasmania, and the great physical distance between them gave Jay hope that it would all subside.

He paused for a moment as if troubled by something. Then he continued, "I went to her house as a friend a few days ago to help out with some tasks, and I find out that the new man has arrived unexpectedly on her doorstep!"

Jay went on to tell me how this new man, who was supposedly abroad, had changed his plans at the last minute, deciding instead to go to her favourite place, which she had spoken so much about, in order to contemplate everything that had happened between them and to work out what she meant to him and what to do about it. "Apparently this new man felt guided to look her up as everything that had happened to him after he had made the decision to go to her favourite place to think just fell uncannily into place for him, leaving him with the feeling that he had made the right decision not to continue his journey abroad."

I was listening intently as Jay explained the details of what had happened: "Apparently this woman turns up out of nowhere, in a bright turquoise van just before a wild storm hits and drives him safely through a storm all the way to Wilsons Promontory. She tells him that he should follow his instincts. Then a few days later, he is sitting in the café, and he is handed a parcel addressed to 'The Swiss man travelling on a pushbike'."

(As it became clear that Jay was now talking about me and that I was unknowingly connected to his story, an electrical sensation was intensifying in my body!)

Jay continued, "And this book is all about chance meetings and following your instincts and convinces him to follow his heart and find her."

Jay had no idea that he was talking about me, and until now, I had no idea that the Swiss man was the man that Jay's previous girlfriend had met on her holiday! Only now did the connections fall into place.

My body became so charged with electricity at the realization of what was happening, that if I had heard another word, I was sure that my hair would stand up! I was so full of electricity that I felt that I was about to explode. Without any explanation to Jay, I bolted out of the house and ran like a maniac at top speed around the block to get rid of all the electricity that had accumulated in my body before returning. As crazy as that seems, it was all that

I could do to get rid of the mounting electrical charge within me and settle back down again!

It is all very interesting:

I meet Jay, and I am incredibly attracted to him.

Jay tells me that I share the birthdate of his previous partner.

Jay shares that his ex fell in love with a man she met on a journey.

I unknowingly pick up the very man that she has fallen in love with.

Unaware of the connection, I advise him to listen to his instincts.

I innocently send him a book that influences his decision to join Jay's ex-partner.

Jay is now on my couch in North Melbourne sharing his devastation.

Listening to Jay, I came to realise how our lives can be intriguingly intertwined.

Jay and I discovered many other coincidental connections in our lives, starting from as early as eight years of age, living in the same town, living just two streets apart and playing in the same paddock. Coincidences are certainly an interesting aspect of life.

It makes me want to giggle with delight at the mysterious, intricate "undercurrents" of our lives. Are we the players in a big soap opera being staged on earth?

A sense of humour is indeed a great treasure to keep at hand.

I could certainly write a whole book on incredible synchronicities that just seem to defy belief, not only of my own, but also those shared by so many other people.

There's my close family friend living in Holland who went camping in Austria and shared a few meals with a German couple camping next to him. Many years later he went camping in France, and the couple camping next to him looked familiar. They approached each other and realised that they had camped side by side in Austria. Later, after another half a lifetime and living in Australia, he is camping in Cairns, in the north of Australia, and to their amazement and disbelief, they recognize each other, this time camping directly opposite each other! It makes me giggle.

Synchronicity? Very interesting! How does that work?

I have had so many synchronicities and serendipities throughout my life that I can no longer just write them off as mere coincidence, and I can no longer believe that proper coincidences even exist at all. There is something far more intriguing going on.

To me, "Oh, what a coincidence" is a good explanation when we don't know how to explain what has just happened. It makes something that feels a trifle confusing or a trifle uncomfortable just a bit more comfortable.

By this stage of my life I have also come to suspect that there is an "external" element of humour, which can somehow interact and play a role in our lives. It has had me in stitches, laughing at both myself, and the things happening around me, with great slapstick affection, many times!

EVENT 17

The Ford Transit Van

ONE OF MY GREATEST treasures was my Toyota HiAce van – a sanctuary, a cocoon into which I could crawl and in which I could remove myself from the penetrating noise of everyday life, escaping into the tranquillity of nature, to bathe in a world of peace all my own.

I had painted it a stunning bright turquoise, and it was always ready to travel, decked out with a comfy mattress, bedding, toiletries, clothes to fit any weather conditions, a stock of supplies, a small stove, and a few pots and pans.

There was only one aspect of my little van that didn't adequately serve my needs and that was the low ceiling height. If I had to spend any length of time keeping dry in bad weather, I would have to do it squatting, sitting, or laying down. I loved my faithful little van, but eventually it was time to upgrade to something more comfortable, a van with a table where I could sit, draw, and write if the weather should turn. A van in which, I could stretch and stand up.

I decided to sell my house and buy a motorhome. When I told a friend that I was going to sell my house, she responded, "What a coincidence; we were just this morning looking at property to invest in. We could buy it from you." Just like that, it was sold!

Within a few weeks, my friends took ownership, and I started looking around for motorhomes in various Melbourne RV outlets, but couldn't find anything that appealed, that was light, spacious, practical, and also visually and aesthetically pleasing. Most vans looked heavy, cramped, boxy, and claustrophobic.

Disillusioned with what was available, I wound down my search to just get on with my life as usual. Instead of spending yet another weekend in Melbourne searching, I decided to go back and stay with my friends in the country.

As I drove into my old town, I was immediately captivated by a van on display in the local car sales yard.

"That's it!"

I had found the van that I was looking for. At once, I was in the office having a chat with the sales rep. "It comes in various colours," he pointed out as he showed me through the new Ford Transit van brochure.

"Do they make a version of this van decked out as a motorhome?" I queried.

"No, but you could buy the basic van and convert it yourself."

"I'd like to have a closer look please. Would you mind showing me?"

He grabbed the key, and we entered the van. I loved it! The shape was visually attractive, and it was spacious: I could stand on my tiptoes with lots of room above my head! It was perfect and had lots of metal cross struts to bolt things onto, and I knew that I didn't need to look any further. I had found my Ford Transit van! My mind spun its creative web and flowed with all of the possibilities: Maybe I can throw a mattress in the back and just bolt down an armchair or two with a table?

"It is a bit dark inside. How easy would it be to replace these side panels with windows?" I asked.

"Windows are optional, and they'll make it to your requirements," he said.

"How much?" was my next question.

"Forty thousand dollars for the basic shell."

It was sadly a bit more than I had hoped. I knew that this was definitely the van I wanted. I thanked the salesman for his time and left, keeping the colourful brochure.

I was excited, I had found my van, even though not a motorhome, but it was more than what I wanted to pay.

How am I going to make this happen? I asked myself.

Full of enthusiasm, I went straight to my friend's house to share the good news, and I bolted in with brochure in hand. "Look!" I excitedly showed her the picture of the van. "This is it! This is the van I want! I found it!"

The weekend passed quickly, and it was time to head back to Melbourne. I worked from Monday morning to late Thursday afternoon giving twenty-four hour care to a delightful ninety-year-old lady suffering from dementia.

Driving back to Melbourne, I kept the picture of the van next to me on the passenger seat, wondering whether I should order the new one with windows or see if I could get a cheaper second-hand one and have it professionally converted. Along the way I bought a copy of *The Trading Post*, a catalogue advertising second-hand items for sale.

The following morning after my client was sitting comfortably in her lounge chair listening to her favourite music, I grabbed the opportunity to scan *The Trading Post*.

"What?" I had to look twice, as I could hardly believe my eyes. I found myself reading the advert over and over again to make sure that I wasn't imagining it. It read: "Ford Transit Motorhome for sale, Twenty-eight thousand dollars."

What?

This was half the price of any other similar motorhomes that I had researched, and it was the exact van that I wanted. *Surely that can't be right!* I almost tripped up bolting to the phone.

What a predicament I was in! I had responsibilities; it was Tuesday early morning and I couldn't leave the house until Thursday afternoon after my replacement arrived, and my experience in the prices of recreational vehicles told me this was a bargain not to be missed, let alone a rare item as well! It was exactly what I wanted. I was concerned that, at that price, it wouldn't last until Thursday.

How was I going to deal with this situation? I couldn't dial that number fast enough!'

Ring-ring ... ring-ring ....

"Hello, Burt speaking."

"Oh, hello, Burt. I have just seen your ad for a Ford Transit motorhome for twenty-eight thousand dollars. Is that correct?"

"Yes that's correct," he replied.

I listened as he gave me a rundown on the vehicle, and it sounded just perfect. The more I heard, the more I wanted it.

"I am really genuinely interested, but I am in a predicament as I am tied up for the next three days. I won't be free until Thursday late afternoon, and I'm concerned that I could possibly lose it to someone else. Do you have any suggestions?"

"You needn't worry, you were lucky to catch us. We are packed and heading off down the coast and won't be back until late Thursday afternoon ourselves."

"Oh, what excellent luck – what a relief! How totally perfect!"

We set a time for a test drive late Thursday afternoon. I felt very good about all that we had discussed, the integrity of the person selling the van, and the van itself.

How fortunate I felt that I had decided not to stay in Melbourne but to head to the country, as I would not have seen the Ford Transit van or bought that paper. How incredibly fortunate that I just managed to catch the sellers before they were leaving and how incredibly fortunate that they were not available until late Thursday afternoon either! What good fortune indeed!

Thursday had finally arrived, and I drove up the driveway to where the van was parked. It looked immaculate. I called out a gentle "Hello", after which Burt came out and shook my hand.

With the passing of a polite greeting, we got straight down to business. He was a gentleman and showed me every inch of the vehicle, inside and out. It was perfect! All I had to do now was test-drive it.

I asked him to take me to the steepest hill possible and then on to a shopping centre to see if I could park it. I eagerly placed myself behind the steering wheel. I was a little nervous; I had never driven anything this big before and expected that it would be like driving a truck. I was pleasantly surprised to find it as easy to drive as my little van, only far more comfortable.

He gave me a warm smile and directed me to a very steep hill, and to my surprise it drove up effortlessly. He then directed me to the main shopping street, and I parked in a normal parking bay within all four lines!

"It feels great," I said. "Direct me for a bit of a drive." Following his instructions, I proceeded to turn right with the greatest of ease, and it all felt like a beautiful dream. I could hardly believe how everything seemed just perfect.

Completing my turn, I was faced with a stunning rainbow, arching over a line of majestic, tall, Kauri pines, through which glistened a row of beautiful yachts anchored amidst dancing diamonds and touched by the glowing warmth of the setting sun. So many of my favourite things!

"Oh my God, look at that! Isn't that just a perfect picture? How stunning!" I remarked as I drove, in awe of the beauty enveloping us.

It was almost too perfect! In fact, I wondered if any of this was real at all.

It just all seemed too good to be true. I started thinking it over in the quiet of my mind: *All I need to do is put some bolts on the inside of the doors so that I can lock it from the inside at night and figure out a way to power my computer. Everything else is just perfect!*

Within seconds, he faced me and said, "There are bolts on the insides of all the doors, and if you wish, I could quite easily get an extra twelve-volt socket put in the dashboard so that you could run a computer."

Well! I nearly had an accident! I couldn't believe what I had just heard! Was this man reading my mind? Bolts? Computer? He *must* have read my mind – or else I was hearing things!

I wanted confirmation. "Did you just say that there were bolts on the insides of the doors and that you could put a socket in the dash for my computer?" I asked.

"Yes, that's right. All the doors have internal bolts, and I would be happy to put a socket in the dash for a computer if you wish." He beamed.

"Thank you, I would greatly appreciate that."

This whole scenario already seemed suspiciously like a dream, but his immediate response to my thoughts once again prompted new questions on my agenda for how life worked. I was usually the one picking up thoughts, but this role reversal took me by surprise.

"I would like to get an RACV check on the vehicle before finalizing a purchase, and if all that checks out, you may consider the van sold." I had found my dream van.

Burt was an amazing man who went far beyond the extra mile. He did everything for me that I requested, including all the red tape. When it was all done, signed, sealed, and paid for, he drove across Melbourne to my location and set aside his entire day just to make sure that the handover went smoothly and that I understood how to operate everything with confidence. The van was in immaculate condition, but not only was I lucky in regard to the van; even the décor of bright turquoise with yellow accents was perfect, along with the big windows in every panel.

This certainly reminded me of the funky buttoned-up jackets scenario: know what you want, and then somehow, mysteriously, the world arranges it for you. Now I had told my friend that I was going to sell my house, and she replied, "What a coincidence; we were just looking to buy a house this morning as an investment" and bought my house. Then my commitments had kept me unavailable to inspect the van but had coincided perfectly with Burt's being away. Then he had responded to my unspoken thoughts by answering them in detail. Beyond that, the experience came packaged with many of my favourite things: rainbows, yachts, the ocean, dancing diamonds, majestic Kauri pines, the warm yellow glow of a setting sun – not to mention Burt, who is my hero: he is meticulous, kind, and helpful way beyond the extra mile.

Life certainly has some interesting twists! I have been shown many times that if we really desire something enough and put our thoughts and attention to it, somehow, sometimes, it can miraculously show up. And as for the picture-perfect rainbows, and the dream settings? They're just the trimmings, but oh, what a delight!

EVENT 18

The Bending of Time

T HERE HAVE BEEN VARIOUS occasions in my life when time just didn't "add up".

The first was at the Traralgon City Swimming Pool when I had departed my body and was floating just below the ceiling looking down at my physical body, and the scene below me had frozen in time.

The second was when the bell had rung to sound the beginning of what was to be a fifty-five minute meditation sitting. I had only just sat down on the cushion and closed my eyes for mere seconds when the bell sounded again to end the fifty-five minute sitting. Where did those fifty-five minutes go?

Another occasion when time as we understand it didn't "add up" was when I was living in a northern suburb of Cairns in Far North Queensland.

I was running late for work at Ellis Beach, where I was due to start at two o'clock. It was a twenty-minute drive, and I always left home at half past one to allow for any unexpected traffic conditions, usually arriving between five or ten minutes early.

I was still at home when I looked at the clock on the wall. To my shock, it showed ten minutes to two o'clock! I checked the time on the microwave, which also showed ten minutes to two o'clock.

A slight panic came over me, as I knew that I was going to be at least ten minutes late if I was lucky enough to have no traffic to deal with. I quickly grabbed my bag, left the house, locked the door, hopped into the car, and turned the engine on. The clock in the dash read nine minutes to two o'clock, and I faced a twenty-minute drive to get to work. The traffic was as busy as usual, and for the first half of the journey I travelled at my normal speed, but during the latter part of the journey, which happened to be a one-lane road without passing lanes, I was stuck behind a truck travelling at only 40 km/h. I resolved that I was going to be at least fifteen minutes late for work.

Miraculously, I arrived at work, and the clock on my dash read two minutes to two o'clock. That meant that I had completed the whole journey from Yorkey's to Ellis Beach in just seven minutes. Not possible! The journey, even if you were speeding the whole way with clear passage, could not possibly be undertaken in seven minutes.

I had completed a twenty-minute drive in seven minutes and had also been stuck behind a very slow truck for the latter part of the journey.

I entered my workplace, immediately checking both the clock on the wall and the clock on the computer. Both clocks confirmed that I had indeed done the physically impossible.

Time had indeed "stretched" to make sure that I got there on time!

Most interesting! *How is that possible?*

From these and other time related experiences that I have had during my life, I had to intellectually accept that there is definitely something about time that just didn't add up. These and other experiences have certainly shown me that time is malleable.

I had to come to terms with the fact that time splits, that time can be both motivated and unmotivated at the same time as in the scenario I experienced at the Traralgon City Pool. I also had to accept that time can simply disappear, as in the loss of the 55 minute meditation sitting and that it can stretch as shown in the event of driving from Yorkey's to Ellis Beach. I continue to question time.

EVENT 19

The Paper Clip Man

I T WAS LATE, AND I had just pulled up the blankets for a good night's sleep when I realised that I had forgotten to prepare an article I needed the following day. Reluctantly, I removed myself from the comforts of my bed and grabbed the first pair of long pants and sleeved top that I could find to keep myself warm.

I was always very conscientious in matching my clothes in both design and colour, but it was late, cold, and unlikely that anyone was going to knock on my door at this time of night. The first items I grabbed happened to be a blue and white polka-dot pant and a multi-coloured striped top. Not like me at all, and it was one of the few times in my life when my clothes were so badly coordinated.

As I put on my clothes, I thought, *This looks awful, but no one will see it.* I shrugged and put them on anyway. Then I opened my computer to the document that I was to prepare.

In those days the Windows program had an inbuilt computer help system, which was the cartoon character of a paper clip with a face. It would randomly pop onto your screen with a caption giving helpful computer-related hints such as "If you are having trouble closing a document, you can hit 'control, alt, delete' to close."

The paper clip man was my hero, and I always took the time to read the helpful hints.

I barely started on my document when the paper clip man appeared on my screen with the caption "Striped pants and polka-dot shirt do not make a good fashion statement."

I gasped and nearly fell off my chair! What could I possibly make of that? What was I to think? Was there a hidden camera in my computer? Was someone from the Windows office looking at me through the computer screen and playing with me? How could I make sense of this?

I took some comfort in the fact that whoever or whatever wrote the statement had gotten the garments the wrong way around. Nevertheless, it did give me a bit of a shock.

The event was placed in the "odd events basket" in the back of my brain, where it lay dormant until almost a decade later when I had semi-committed to travelling to Burma with a group of people, and the deadline had arrived to make the full commitment and pay the deposit. I was very eager to go, but all day I'd been plagued by constant thoughts and mental pictures of dirty water, poor hygiene, and negative health effects.

I was in turmoil between my genuine desire to go and my constant mental warnings of dirty water that just wouldn't go away.

By late evening, I was still unsure what to do, but I couldn't delay my responsibility any longer and had to make a decision.

I opened my computer to find an email from the person organising the trip asking about my decision. I was now sitting in the position to return my reply, but I was still at a loss as to which decision to make when up popped the paper clip man!

The caption read: "Do not dive into murky waters."

Once again, I gasped and nearly fell off my chair!

Needless to say, I made the decision not to go ahead with the trip.

After their return from Burma, I heard their stories of how sick they had become throughout their visit and that some had become quite seriously ill.

I had by now come to terms with the fact that time can shrink, bend, stretch, freeze, and maybe even overlap on itself, possibly explaining how one could see into future events, and that we have physical bodies, as well as energy bodies; that our personalities are not confined to the physical body; and that more than one personality can actually inhabit one body at the same time; and that we transmit and receive information through wavelength frequencies, we can instantly feel an event occurring in a far distant place without having any prior knowledge of it, and that something that we strongly desire can somehow miraculously be presented to us.

I remain undoubtedly convinced that we are all intimately connected and know each other but seem to be unaware of this, that there are things happening around us that are beyond our human frequency range which we can neither hear nor see, that we are possibly influenced from another dimension that we cannot register, that the events of our lives are recorded, and that even our date of death may be pre-set.

I had come to grasp and accept, through my own first-hand experiences, that these things are just as much a real part of my life as is sitting in a café and having a cappuccino. But here I was, now faced with the mystery of the paper clip man!

The two incidents with the paper clip man differed: The first event involved what I was physically wearing, which caused me to wonder if there was an inbuilt camera in my computer and someone in some computer office somewhere was watching. That seemed most unlikely but almost feasible. But the second event had to do with what was going on in my thoughts, and that in itself was a far greater challenge to ponder.

My search for a logical explanation could only come up with the notion that there had to be another dimension from where our thoughts could be intercepted and through which our lives can be guided and influenced. How else can that be explained? The events where Tim saves me twice, in different countries when my life was in danger certainly backs up this conclusion. I am still yet to find any other logical explanation.

EVENT 20

The Pencil Appears

I was living in Yulara, a resort village near Uluru (Ayers Rock) in the middle of the Simpson Desert. The nearest town was Alice Springs, a four-hour drive away. Choice of supplies at Yulara was very limited, and if you needed to get something specific, you had to drive the 450 kilometres to 'Alice'.

Just about to head off to work, I receive a phone call from my mother. "Mum, sorry, I can't talk. I have to race off to work," I explain as I try to dress with the phone in hand.

"Is there anything you need?" she enquires.

Immediately the pencil springs to mind. I had been wanting a pencil for sketching, one that lets me extend the lead as it gets used, houses extra leads inside, and has a rubber on the end. I couldn't buy one in Yulara, and it was a long drive to Alice Springs.

As much as I wanted the pencil, I also suspected that it might cause a hassle for my mother, as it was more likely to be found in an art supply shop rather than the average news agency. Not wanting to cause her any difficulties, I decide not to ask.

"No, thanks for asking, Mum, but I have everything that I need," and we say our goodbyes.

As I keep dressing and getting ready for work, a battle rages inside my head: "Ring her back. Get the pencil." – "No, she has enough to do." – "Get the pencil!" – "No, leave her be."

This battle continues throughout the whole process of dressing and getting my things together for work until finally, I make the clear decision not to bother my mother and let the idea of the pencil go.

I bolt down the stairwell and step onto the soft red sand in front of me – and there lies the pencil that I had held in my mind just moments before.

Shiny as brand new.

Not a scratch to be found.

Full of new leads.

Complete with rubber that has never been used.

This is just another example of things that we desire, often somehow mysteriously showing up. I had a very strong sense at the time that the fact that I *genuinely* put my mother's interests before my own, had made a difference to the pencil appearing or not.

It was just another interesting moment among so many that continues to force me to question the very essence of our lives.

EVENT 21

Our Thoughts Affect Others

I HAD ALREADY LEARNT AND experienced so many abstract aspects of life that just didn't fit in with mainstream beliefs that at times I wondered about who I was and where I fitted in. I struggled a great deal with this throughout my life.

At times I even doubted myself and wondered if I was normal at all. But it was never long before another event would be thrown at me, confirming previous thoughts as I endeavoured to decipher and understand the bigger picture.

I had already experienced and realised that we are all somehow intimately connected to each other but that most of us live as if we are totally unaware of it. I knew that we are receivers and transmitters, and our thoughts must therefore on some level affect every other person and therefore the whole of the human race in some way.

This was verified again when I had purchased a new address book as my old one was falling apart. It was a laborious task copying my contacts from the old to the new in my obsessively neat handwriting. I had reached the *S* section, and my writing hand was starting to cramp up so I decided to stop for the day and take the dog for a walk to the oval across the road.

Dog on lead, I locked the house and the front gate and began to amble across the road.

The last entry had been a person by the name of Geoff Stamford whom I had not seen or communicated with since college days, twenty years earlier, except for bumping into each other one afternoon almost a decade earlier and exchanging our contact details.

Since putting the pen down I had held that person in my thoughts, wondering how his life was going, what he was up to and his whereabouts and even if his contact details were still relevant.

I had a sudden urge to go back to the house to get my mobile phone, even though I didn't usually carry it with me when I was taking the dog for a walk. It was a strong urge, so I decided to follow it through.

I turned around, went back, unlocked the gate, unlocked the house, retrieved my phone, relocked the house, relocked the gate, and started across the road.

Ring-ring ....

"Hello, Viviana speaking."

"Hi there, Viviana. It's Geoff Stamford here. I just had a strong urge to call you and see what you are up to these days."

We are always transmitting and receiving. This is just more proof that our thoughts affect each other whether we intend them to or not – and whether or not we are even aware of it.

Unfortunately, for the most part we seem to be totally unaware of this.

I have long observed, when watching science fiction films with "way out" ideas set in some future time, how many of these ideas come into reality.

When I was younger, I thought that our brains were somewhat like sponges and that the brain absorbed and reflected back whatever you personally subjected it to.

I have now come to believe that our own individual world is not created by our own singular thoughts alone. Rather, to a greater extent, it is a mix of everyone's combined thought processes that presents to us the world that we perceive to be real.

Simply put, I believe that our world is somehow the result of both our individual and combined thinking rather than the result of our individual thinking. Therefore, it is crucially important that regardless of whatever we have experienced, we take global responsibility and think positive thoughts for humanity because our thoughts are indeed individually powerful and affect everyone.

I believe that it is imperative that what we are subjected to through television, film, the media, radio, newspapers, and politics, be of positive rather than negative coverage if we wish to live in a happy, uplifting and positive world.

Having witnessed the incredible power of thought I can only suggest that thought needs to be used gently and wisely with greater respect and attention to detail if we are to *positively* evolve. We need to be mindful of our thinking process and what we focus upon. Referring back to the world of science fiction as an example, if our unified thoughts do indeed create the world that we experience, than the greater number of people around the globe watching and focusing on a particular film, the more likely that the events in that film will become our unified reality.

Even though we mostly come from our conditioned selves according to what we have experienced in this physical life, the goal to elevate our thinking for the good of all is a worthy goal and one that I believe matters more than any other. I remember a wise elderly woman's response to my mentioning something negative when she confronted me in my tracks and said, "Stop! I am not interested in negatives. There's negative and positive in everything. It is easy to find the negatives, but they do not lift the soul. Give me something positive, and I will show interest in listening."

I have never forgotten her wise words, and I continue to endeavour to elevate my thinking. It is never easy changing ingrained patterns of thinking from the past, but I believe it is imperative to continually keep working on ourselves, and our thoughts, if we wish to create a better world to live in. I have come to believe that each thought plays a role in our overall unified experience and each and every one of us adds their 'flavour' to what we become.

EVENT 22

Min Min Lights?

ENJOYING A LONG WALK through the dense rainforest with a friend near Mossman Gorge, I had a strong sense of "something else" as we passed by a particular spot. At the first polite opportunity, I cut into the conversation with "Sorry to stop you in your tracks but I just need to go back along the path a little and take another look."

We went back a short distance, and I had the same feeling. I couldn't see anything. I decided to take a photo in the direction of the feeling and turned back to my friend and continued on our walk.

When I returned home, I downloaded my photos onto my computer and browsed through.

When I came to the photo where I had "sensed" something but saw nothing, there were two very distinct balls of light in the picture.

My first thought was; *that's odd; my camera has never done that before*, thinking that there was a problem with my camera. But as I continued to view my photos, they were all perfect, and no such balls of light appeared on any other pictures.

I had seen dim spots on other people's digital photos before and thought that the spots were just dust particles in the air with the light reflecting off them, but these were very bright, much more distinct, and strikingly large, the size of tennis balls.

Thinking that there would be a logical explanation, I thought it must be just dewdrops and that the flash had somehow bounced off them. I enlarged the photo for a closer look.

Once it was enlarged, I could clearly see that these two balls of light were suspended in midair and didn't touch anything at all. Both balls of bright, white light, had a slight pale bluish type of energy field around them.

What on earth am I looking at here? I was intrigued and wondered if I was ever going to figure this world out.

This was new to me, and again I was challenged.

I recalled a conversation about Min Min lights with an indigenous Australian lady, many years earlier, who explained that she didn't walk through certain forest areas at night because of the mischievous Min Min lights, personalities in the form of balls of light which would chase after her through the forest.

I also remembered another lady who had said that she studied energy fields, and I had kept her details, so I decided to look her up and show her the photo.

"Oh, they're orbs," she explained.

"What are orbs?" I was intrigued.

"Orbs are personalities and come in the form of balls of light energy." She continued, "I became interested in orbs myself after my father had passed away and I was spending Christmas at my mother's place. I sensed something in the room, but there wasn't anything to see, so I grabbed my camera and took a photo. When I looked at the photo, there was a ball of light, about the size of a tennis ball, suspended in air, next to my mother's elbow. I took more photos, and they showed that the ball of light kept following my mother around the room. I personally think that it was my father's energy." She went on to say, "I have a file full of orb pictures."

It occurred to me that this certainly fitted in with my own experience that the personality didn't take up the whole physical body space and that if the personality was indeed only the size of a tennis ball, the body space could accommodate more than one personality as in the events that I had experienced with the deceased aboriginal boy and my deceased father.

I was grateful for her time and explanation and didn't think much more about it until one day, years later, when I became a personality inside a ball of my own, which I will discuss further into the book.

Life is indeed very, very, interesting.

EVENT 23

I'm Now in the Future

I HAD A VERY STRONG vision flash in front of me whilst sipping a cup of tea in my apartment in the Simpson Desert, in the centre of Australia.

It wasn't like a usual daydream or exercise of my imagination. The difference was that this picture that flashed before me was accompanied by an unquestionable "knowing" that I was looking at a real event that hadn't yet taken place.

In this visual flash, I saw myself dressed all in white – a white long and flowing cotton skirt and a white cotton top. I looked extremely happy, enjoying the sunshine as I walked along a stunning beach beside the ocean. Just in front of me was a huge, sun-bleached piece of driftwood, a large section of a washed-up tree that I was just about to navigate around – and as quickly as the flash came, it left me.

I was living in the dry, red sandy desert near Uluru at the time, so it was quite a surprise to see this vision. As I usually did when these odd events happened in my life, I rang my good friend Enna. Enna was always fascinated by the events that I encountered and was ready to listen, respectfully, without judgement, every time. She also remembered the many things that I had shared with her, and she was like a checklist for my sanity.

As always, I explained the vision to her in detail.

A couple of years passed, and the memories of that vision had faded away with time. I moved to Alice Springs, still surrounded in every direction by the desert. Then I travelled the gulf country and eventually moved to Cairns, where I purchased a seaside property just two streets back from a stunning beach. I walked along that beautiful beach every day, and it was always visually impressive. I felt extremely lucky to be there.

One day I went for my regular walk along the beach and was confronted by something different. My path ahead was obstructed by a huge, sun-bleached piece of driftwood that had been washed up on the beach overnight. It was a large section of a tree, and I was going to have to navigate around it. I was delighted to see it, as I loved the smooth texture of driftwood and this was by far the most impressive piece I had ever seen. I continued to walk towards it until …

Flashback!

Oh my God! I'm in that very picture!

I had reached the point of distance between myself, and the driftwood just as it was in the visual flash all those years ago!

It was no surprise as I looked down at my clothes to see that I was wearing a white cotton top and a flowing white cotton skirt.

I couldn't get home fast enough, and excitedly, I rang Enna;

"Enna, do you remember that I had a vision of me walking on a beach –"

I didn't have to say another word. Enna had a great memory and knew within a moment the vision that I had shared with her a few years earlier. She cut in, "Yes, I remember. You were wearing white, and there was a big piece of driftwood in front of you." Enna remembered and it always gave me great comfort when she did.

I remembered back to the thought that had flashed in front of me on my arrival at the shopping centre near Uluru when a matter-of-fact statement flashed through my mind: *I'm going to be working here one day.* I had ignored, discounted, and forgotten about it until one day, years later, I was working in that exact place. I had also suddenly remembered and recognised what I had known many years prior to it coming to fruition.

This was not a déjà vu situation. This was a scene witnessed many, many years before the event and was so prominent that it was shared long before it happened.

What I found really interesting about this was that I was in that same identical frame of the "moving picture" of my life at two separate times, many years apart.

Or rather, let me just repeat that: I saw moments of my future life, as if in a frame caught on a roll of film, which eventually materialized many years later when I caught up with it properly.

So personally, I have learnt that somehow future moments are pre-set for us to experience. I had always thought that we had free will, but at this stage of my life I was still left wondering if we have any free will at all. Are all our moments pre-set, or are just some pre-set? What is really going on here? Certainly a lot more than I could fathom.

I had by this stage experienced many levels and varied aspects to our existence and had to deduce that we are indeed multifaceted beings and that each facet united in the physical body to carry out its own unique part to play in our overall human experience.

How truly incredible we really are.

EVENT 24

EVENT 24

Wonderful Serendipity

LOOKING FOR A PARTICULAR book, I drove to the local bookshop, only to be told that it was out of print and unlikely to be printed again.

As I drove off further down the road, I caught sight of a sign reading "Second-Hand Bookshop".' I had never noticed it before and immediately decided to pop in and try my luck there.

I was overwhelmed by the sight of thousands of books lining the walls and filling the aisles of bookcases rising up out of the floor. I felt small among the towering shelves and was left wondering how on earth I was going to find the book that I wanted amongst the multitude of written material.

I was obviously going to need assistance.

There was no one at the counter, so I proceeded to walk through the aisles to see if I could find someone to ask. In the third aisle I came across a lady, sitting on the ground, sorting out a huge pile of books strewn on the floor in front of her.

I approached her, getting as close to her as possible and stopping only when my big toe had connected with the pile of books blocking the aisle between us.

"Hi. You have an amazing amount of books in here," I remarked.

"Yes, what can I do for you?" she replied.

"Well, I'm looking for a particular book, and I was wondering if you might have a copy." I gave her the name of the book.

"I vaguely recollect that I may have seen it somewhere, but to be honest, I wouldn't know where to begin to look for it at this stage. As you can see, looking down at the books, I have more books than I can get sorted."

In turn I also looked down at the mountain of books below to find that all the while we had been conversing, the book that was touching my big toe was the very book that I had come in to purchase.

"Oh wow, here it is," I said, moving my foot and bending down to pick it up.

"Now that's serendipity if I ever saw it!" she said with surprise.

"You will have to autograph that in the book," I said with a giggle.

She did just that, and we both had great smiles on our faces as I walked out carrying my book.

I have noticed that these coincidences are common, and yet each time they occur we seem very surprised, amazed, as if these coincidences are almost unbelievable. They also certainly give us a boost of delightful energy each time!

As I have consistently experienced these coincidences throughout my life, I have noticed that although they can occur at any emotional stage, the occurrences have always accelerated when I am in my most happy, contented times and especially when I live in awareness and gratitude for everything that I have, both in the material sense and the non-material sense.

For instance, I've been grateful for something as simple as being able to have a shower as well as being grateful for the skills that I have been given.

When consciously and genuinely practicing this state of grace and gratitude, it is almost as if the universe sends me little gifts, as if thanking me straight back.

Too often I fall back into conditioned patterns and forget to live with gratitude; during those times, coincidences certainly diminish. I have no doubt that living in gratitude plays a very important role in elevating our world and our own life experience.

EVENT 25

Need Signature Now

H AVING NOT LONG BEEN in Cairns, Queensland, I had just completed a real estate agents course, and all I had left to do before beginning my new career was to have two passport ID photos printed and signed on the back by someone who had known me for more than twenty years.

The photos were not a problem, but where in Queensland was I going to find someone who had known me for that long? Anyone who knew me for that long would be thousands of kilometres away.

Wanting to do the right thing, I was faced with a bit of a dilemma.

The photos were going to take a week to be processed, so for the next seven days, my thoughts focused on how I was going to manage to get someone to sign my documents.

The week flew by quickly, and the photographer rang to say that the photos were ready, so off I went to pick them up. I walked out of the shop opening the envelope to see how the photos had turned out. Happy with the result, I put them back into the envelope, thinking: *Now, who can I get to sign the back of these photos to complete the process?*

I looked up from the envelope and my eyes fell immediately upon an ex-boss of mine from Victoria. I had worked for him on five separate occasions in the last twenty years, and he just happened to be on holiday in Queensland. Problem solved!

There are far too many of these events in my life to just label them as coincidences and brush them aside.

Whilst I was living near Uluru, these serendipitous events were happening at such an amazing rate that I decided to keep a record of them. I constantly carried a notebook and couldn't write fast enough. Eventually I had to stop because I started to get repetitive strain injury (RSI) in my hand from all the speed notes that I was writing.

Life is so much bigger than we think it is. When we can start to break through the layers of conditioning that we have all been subjected to throughout our physical lives, and the belief that there is just physical birth, physical life and physical death, we can start to glimpse the wider panorama, and life becomes truly amazing.

EVENT 26

The Hot Air Balloon

A T 4.15 A.M. ON a pitch black night, I waited at the curb in expectation of an exciting adventure. I didn't have to wait long before the courtesy bus arrived to pick me up for an early morning hot air balloon ride. I boarded the bus, and the driver informs us that the journey to the balloon location is to take approximately an hour. After a welcome, introduction, and schedule rundown, he turns off the lights to allow us to catch up on some sleep for the duration of the drive.

I rested my head against the window, and the rhythmic pulse of the motor caressed me to sleep almost immediately.

I am now high up in the hot air balloon with six other people. The pilot is chatting away to his attentive passengers, and the view below is stunning. Like birds in flight looking down at the world, we scan the hills and lush green pastures below. Although seemingly motionless, we navigate over farmhouses resembling toy houses on a monopoly board and watch them disappear into the distance in no time at all.

Whilst the pilot is chatting and holding the attention of the other passengers, I look up into the striking bright red and orange colours of the balloon above and notice the morning sky showing through a large rip in the balloon.

That doesn't look good, I'm thinking as I continue to watch the split in the balloon. I can see that the edges of the split are starting to flap more vigorously and that the rip is getting bigger. I can see that we are in a dangerous predicament.

This doesn't look good at all. How are we going to handle this one? I silently ask myself.

Realising that I need to alert the pilot without causing group panic, I wriggle away from the middle of the group to the back of the group so that whilst everyone is looking at the pilot, no one can see what I am doing.

To get the pilot's attention, whilst no one can see me, I wave vigorously with one hand whilst pointing up into the balloon with the other hand.

The young pilot catches on and continues to chat to the others whilst discreetly checking out what I am pointing to. He sees the state of the balloon above.

Without a word to the others, he looks at me in appreciative acknowledgement as I witness the rosy colour in his cheeks turn a pale shade of grey. Obviously he knows the predicament that we are in. I watch him try to continue as normal, and at the same time, he scans the ground below to find his options for a solution.

I look up again and see that the rip is now twice as long. I return my gaze to the young pilot and see his expression of concern. I'm not sure that he is equipped to handle the situation, and we are still quite high up.

"We're here, everyone," the coach driver announced as he flicked on the interior lights.

I was greatly relieved to realize that I had just had a vivid dream.

As I stretched my body out of sleeping position, I looked out of the window to see a line of six balloon baskets lying on their sides, their balloons attached and spread out along the ground in front of them, waiting be filled with hot air from the flaming gas bottles. It was a magnificent sight to watch the different coloured balloons fill up and eventually lift their baskets to an upright position.

The bus passengers were divided into six groups. Each group was allotted a balloon and guided to stand in front of their allotted baskets in readiness to embark.

All the balloons departed, one by one, just minutes apart, but our balloon hadn't inflated at all and was still lying on the ground. Once having attended to the departure of all the other balloons, the land crews came over to inspect ours.

Eventually a crew member came over to our small group, who by now were feeling somewhat deserted as we watched all the other balloons fly off into sunrise, to explain the hold-up. "Really sorry about the slight delay, folks. As you can see for yourselves, the balloon is not inflating, so we need to remove it and replace it with another. We should be in the air within half an hour."

Whilst he drove off to get another balloon, the other crew members continued to survey the balloon to figure out why it wasn't inflating. Eventually they found the problem: the top of the balloon had a large rip in it.

It is amazing what our dreams can tell us. I remember when I first started renovating my first house. I had no experience whatsoever in plastering, building, hanging doors, laying bricks, building cupboards, and all those other skills waiting to be discovered. After a while, though, I figured out that if I came upon a problem that I really couldn't solve, if I could simply let it go unanswered, in most cases I would be shown what to do in a dream that night. The next morning, upon waking, I would remember the dream and think: *oh, so that's how it's done!* I have no doubt that somehow, our consciousness continues functioning whilst our physical body sleeps.

As for the hot air balloon, I was left with a huge question mark. In past events I had often witnessed seeing the future as a flash, in daytime, long before it happened. In those events, the vision correlated identically, leading me to believe that time bends.

However, this was different. This was not a seeing of the exact future at all. In the dream, I was physically up in the air, yet in physical reality I never got into the ripped balloon at all. In the physical, the balloon was ripped in the same spot as in my dream.

How does this all logically piece together? Does our organic physical body need rest in order to replenish itself whilst our consciousness continues to function and even gather information for us in some way whilst the body sleeps? How does one explain this?

It is certainly rather intriguing.

EVENT 27

Pennies from Heaven

I HAD JUST PURCHASED ANOTHER "renovator's delight" property for a bargain price. The property, inscribed with black and red graffiti on the inside walls, was in poor repair. I loved a challenge, and I couldn't wait to let my creativity transform the property into a lovely home.

It certainly needed some intense cleaning and painting before I could even entertain the thought of moving in, so the first task was to wash all the floors and walls.

I scrubbed the floor and washed the walls, and whilst the white floor tiles, which now gleamed, were drying, I started getting everything ready to paint the walls and ceilings.

The back bedroom was the first room to dry and was now ready for painting.

I walked into the room with the paint tin and noticed something in the middle of the floor. Having just washed the floor, and being very particular in my cleaning, I was a bit surprised to see anything on the floor at all. *Looks like a coin*, I thought as I walked to the centre of the room to see what it was.

How did I miss a five-cent piece in the middle of the room? I picked it up from the floor. I certainly never carry money in my pockets as I always keep my money in a purse in my handbag, so it couldn't have fallen out of my clothing, and no one else had been in the property.

I was too busy to be contemplating the mystery of the five-cent piece, so I shrugged it off and placed the coin on the kitchen windowsill.

Walls and ceilings painted, I took a short break in the lounge room with a cup of tea and then entered the second bedroom with paint tin in hand. Once again there was what looked like another five-cent piece right in the centre of the shiny white tiled floor. *Now that is a bit odd*, I thought as I strolled to have a look. Sure enough, it was indeed another five-cent piece right in the middle of the newly scrubbed floor!

I placed the second coin next to the first coin on the windowsill and returned to paint the room.

I finished renovating for the day and decided to go and visit a friend. As I headed down the path, I found another five-cent piece. I didn't think much about the third coin because it could have easily just fallen out of someone's pocket, but the first two coins were a bit of a puzzle.

I moved into my new abode and found a job working at a car rental company that entailed a great variety of tasks including delivering vehicles, filling out contracts, detailing cars, and checking cars for damage.

Each time I detailed a vehicle, I would find a coin in the strangest of places – caught in the radio rim, centred underneath the carpet, or lodged in some obscure part of the car where coins wouldn't normally fall. I didn't ascribe much importance to them, but as I found more and more coins, the line of mostly five-cent pieces on my kitchen windowsill was forming a rather long chain, spanning the length of the glass pane within just a few weeks.

A traveller moved into the spare room for a short stay and on the first night shared an odd experience with me. "I had a really weird experience" he said. "I was taking a shower, and I heard the sound of something dropping in the shower cubicle, so I looked down and saw a ten-cent piece lying on the floor of the shower. It sounded as if it dropped from the ceiling, so I looked up, but all I saw was just the plaster ceiling and nowhere that it could have fallen from."

He continued, "I know that it was definitely not there when I entered the shower and I was totally naked so it couldn't have fallen from me." He looked perplexed. He had only just moved in that day. After his experience, I explained the chain of coins on the kitchen windowsill and how they kept turning up in the weirdest of places.

The experience had made him a little uncomfortable, which I found to be a normal reaction whenever logical explanations can't be found, and there were no more coin events during the rest of his stay.

One day I had to deliver a car to a couple on holiday from England. After completing the paperwork, we began inspecting the car for any existing damage before handing over the keys.

As we were inspecting the vehicle, we were suddenly all stopped by the sound of metal clinking seven metres further down the driveway. We turned to see a piece of silver metal glistening in the sun, about a metre above the ground, and watched it fall back to earth again. It had obviously been dropped on the concrete and had bounced to where it was when we saw it.

We all instantly looked up to see what could possibly have dropped it. We were amused to find that there was absolutely nothing above us that could have dropped it. We searched the sky for a bird or plane, but there was nothing to see other than clear blue sky without even a hint of cloud. The nearest building was forty or more metres away from this long driveway. There were no trees or bushes nearby, and with a clear view out to the road, there was no traffic or any people to be seen.

"Pennies from heaven," said the Englishman, scratching his head in confusion.

"Where on earth did that come from?" asked his wife looking around for an answer, rather dismayed.

"Interesting," I replied, secretly chuckling to myself.

The three of us had walked over to the piece of metal that now lay on the concrete driveway to discover that it was a twenty-cent piece.

"Would you mind if I kept this?" I asked them.

"Not at all," they replied, still confused by the event.

When the week had passed, on picking up the vehicle I asked them what conclusions they had come to in regard to the twenty-cent coin.

"Oh it must have been a bird," the Englishman replied.

"It obviously rolled out of the gutter," his wife concluded.

Their conclusions were the best that they had been able to come up with, even though at the time, we were unable to see any birds, and the gutter was more than eight metres away.

I could see by their reaction that there was really no point sharing the experience of my growing coin collection.

I have learnt that generally people need to find logical, practical 'physical' conclusions to their experiences in order to somehow reaffirm their sanity. If a logical physical conclusion can't be found, then most often they simply deny the event or conjure up a logical-sounding explanation to ease the discomfort of mystery. It's as if any experience that fails to provide a logical answer must therefore go hand in hand with insanity – sanity being a comfort zone and insanity being outside of our comfort zone.

The more these events are openly shared, the more likely we are to be able to move forwards and embrace that we are much more than what we *think* we are, more than what we *have been taught to believe that we are.*

We may even discover that what we *believe in* plays a direct role in our level of evolution and by denying the truth of our experience, I believe that we are also, to some degree, denying our evolution.

Where did all those coins come from? Were they gifts from another dimension?

If I was able to manifest things myself, I would be winning the lottery every week, feeding the poor, tending the sick, and generally assisting in positive evolution. I have certainly tried focusing on winning the lottery and failed, yet many times I have been given what I have so greatly desired in the most bizarre ways. How does this work?

Is there a centre of control that decides what we are given and what we are not given? A centre of control that knows our innermost desires and has free will to intercept our lives and grant us what we want, providing it fits in with a particular agenda?

As far as I understand at this stage of my life, thinking back to Tim who saved me from danger in two different countries at two different times, the pencil, the funky jackets, and many, many other events, I revisit the thought that other dimensions exist from which energetic forces can somehow penetrate and affect our human dimension. This would certainly explain some of my unexplainable events.

There are still many questions to the great puzzle begging for understanding.

EVENT 28

A Tiny Little Kombi Van

"Yeah, they were really great days according to my parents, and I often listen with a big grin on my face to their wonderful stories," said the young photographer. "At the end of their storytelling sessions I'm always wishing that I could have lived in that era myself. I envy those who did. I reckon I missed out!" His face reflected a daze of wishful thinking.

It was just after the turn of the twenty-first century, and he and I were talking about the changing eras that people experience throughout their lives, but we didn't get much further than the late nineteen sixties and early nineteen seventies. The young photographer had a real fascination for that time period and seemed to know a lot more about the time than I did, even though, like his parents, I lived through it.

He continued, "I know that VW kombi vans were the norm, and my mum and dad had one too. They've got heaps of photo albums, and I love looking through them. Just about every photo includes their old VW kombi van, and they're either hanging out of it, sleeping in it, on top of it, underneath it, or painting something on it. Hilarious, a real eye-catcher, covered in rainbows, massive flowers, ban-the-bomb logos, make-love-not-war graffiti, peace signs, and had a very big, comfortable mattress in the back, buried under a pile of clothes just thrown in. They would drive from one music festival to the next, and when there was no festival, they'd be hanging out with friends doing the same! According to them, life was pretty fantastic, very simple, relaxed and easy compared to these days," he finished.

We ended our conversation as the bus back to town rolled in and we said our goodbyes. Whilst travelling on the bus, my own fun memories poured through my mind. I too had once had a Kombi van with a mattress in the back. I reminisced about the days of rainbow T-shirts, flower power, when "make love, not war" dominated the airwaves, and the masses were demanding peace, marching with banners through the streets in a time when lots of people showed an active interest in protesting against war and were prepared to hold politicians to account.

I felt really grateful that I was one of the lucky ones who had indeed been able to experience and take part in that rather special time.

I exited the bus with thoughts of my own adventures in the Kombi van still in mind and headed to the door of the shopping centre when I glanced to my left towards a telephone booth and saw something sitting on the little shelf below the phone.

Someone has left something behind on the shelf, I thought as I went over to see what it was.

When I got to the phone booth I could hardly contain my laughter! *The universe really does have a great sense of humour,* I thought as I saw what it was.

It was a miniature, orange coloured toy VW Kombi-van, complete with rainbow sticker and "ban the bomb" sign on it. I had a really good chuckle …

I have often found that amidst its tragedies, the universe around us also has a great sense of humour, and I often wonder if we are like a bunch of toddlers being affectionately watched from somewhere beyond our understanding and often, given little gifts to delight us. For I have indeed had a constant supply. Correct or not, it does serve to remind me to enjoy the mystery and not to take life too seriously as we so often do.

EVENT 29

Fate

M Y MOTHER WAS DUE to arrive in a week's time to stay with me in Cairns for the winter months. I was really excited and looking forward to spending some quality time together with her.

As I read a book in the lounge room at home, a picture of my mother falling into the shower recess suddenly flashed across my mind.

Wow! That was a really vivid picture, I thought, so I decided to put my book down and have a look at my bathroom to see what might possibly cause her to fall. I had already learnt that these sorts of pictorial flashes were not to be ignored, however *illogical* they seemed to be.

I looked down at the floor in front of the shower recess where I had placed a wooden slatted bath mat. Knowing that my mother wasn't accustomed to using one of those, I removed it to the side of the shower recess and pushed it into the corner so that there was no way she could fall over it. To make doubly sure that all would be well and safe for her, I placed the clothes hoist over the top of it so that she would have to walk around it. I felt confident that there was nothing else to attend to and that the bathroom was now totally safe.

The week flew by, and Mum had settled into the spare room. It was great to see her, and we were delighted to be in each other's company once again. We spent the evening planning all the wonderful things that we would do together during her stay, and after Mum's full day of travel, she retired early for a good night's sleep.

Crash! Bang!

Mum screamed from the bathroom, and I bolted in to see what had happened. I found her on the floor holding her wrist.

"Mum, what happened?" I asked as I checked her for possible injury.

"I fell over that stupid wooden bathmat!" she exclaimed.

I couldn't believe it! I had taken such great care to push it into a corner and to ensure that it was out of the way and not possible to fall over! Even the clothes hoist that I had placed over it took up more floor space both in width and length than the wooden bath mat.

Mum's wrist was badly bruised but thankfully not broken. The glass shower screen was smashed and had to be replaced. I was left totally dumbfounded in trying to understand this event. Mum would have had to get her foot twenty-five centimetres in and under the clothes hoist in order to have connected with the wooden bath mat, and that would have been a feat on its own, let alone trip over it as well.

This event really left me questioning whether we were indeed subject to "fate" and, for whatever reason, had to undergo certain experiences. Even though we believe that we have free choice, this event certainly joined a long list of questions in my thinking process.

I saw this event happen a week prior to its happening. I figured out the possibilities and removed the cause in order to prevent the incident from occurring. It still happened.

Once more I had to question whether we have a pre-set program and everything is predetermined and whether or not free will truly exists. It seems that my mother had to fall in the bathroom no matter how much I tried to prevent it. So where does free will come in? Are we fated to experience certain events? And if free will doesn't exist, then what is the purpose of life and the evolution thereof? Are we simply just vessels through which life can experience itself?

My brain was taking quite a beating trying to figure this all out, and I so missed having someone in my life with knowledge and practical experience to talk to who could give me some logical answers.

EVENT 30

Mum Falls into Gutter

WE HAD JUST WALKED out of the supermarket and headed to our car, which was parked beside the footpath in front of us.

I was walking a couple of metres ahead of my mother in readiness to unlock the passenger side door for her.

I put the key into the door and was about to turn it when a picture of my mother falling into the gutter flashed in front of my mind's eye.

In response, I immediately pulled the key out of the door and turned to face my mother, who wasn't paying any attention to where she was walking and was instead fumbling for something inside her handbag.

"Mum, be careful," I warned her. "It is a deep step down into the gutter here. Watch where you are going."

"Yeah, yeah," she replied.

Having warned her and heard her reply, I turned to the car and inserted the key. Before I could turn it to open the door, I heard the commotion of my mother falling into the gutter. Mum had broken her ankle and was writhing in pain.

I was again left contemplating whether certain events were preordained, pre-programmed, and destined to be experienced, for whatever reason, regardless of what action we might take to avoid them. Seeing events before they occur has to mean that on some level, our life is most certainly preordained. And if past, present and future already exist, then time itself has to be questionable and life itself becomes even far more intriguing!

237

EVENT 31

Prawns at Popples

ONE OF MY FAVOURITE pastimes was to hang out at Popples, a popular seaside café, reading the newspaper, whilst devouring a plate of garlic prawns, all the while surrounded by the sounds of seagulls, children playing, and the usual café chatter. It was always a pleasant contrast from the silence I normally chose to surround myself with. So, feeling the need for something to eat as I was driving through town, I thought that I would go to Popples and treat myself to garlic prawns for lunch.

"Do not eat prawns at Popples!"

Wow! A very loud, *male*, authoritarian, demanding voice audibly warned and ordered me not to eat prawns at Popples.

It gave me a huge shock. I was totally alone in the car with the windows closed, the air conditioner on, and the radio switched off.

This incredibly authoritarian *male* voice came from everywhere, both within my body and outside of my body, as if permeating the whole space around me and through me.

What and who was that? I asked myself.

I have always been a very self-determined person, not easily influenced by anything or anyone. I have a touch of rebel in my genes and a great dislike for anything authoritarian.

I continued to drive to Popples in defiance, and whilst driving, I entered into dialogue with whatever had spoken to try to figure out what had just occurred.

"What or who are you? You haven't even bothered to introduce yourself! How do I know whether or not I should listen to you? Please explain."

Here I was, driving down the road, speaking to something that I had just heard but couldn't see. I wondered if I had just gone a touch mad.

"If you can interfere with this life and know what I am about to do, then surely you also know something about my personality and who I am and that I don't take orders from just anybody without a good explanation or good understanding of the reasons. So why are you giving me orders? – and please explain who you are." I was no sheep to blindly follow, and so I demanded a reply, still heading towards Popples and looking forward to those mouth-watering garlic prawns.

No reply was forthcoming, so I repeated, "If you are real and you can invisibly watch my life and know what I am about to do, then you should know that my personality also needs you to explain yourself to me, or I will not take heed of what you say. So please introduce yourself, and tell me why I should not eat prawns at Popples and why I should take any notice of you."

Still no reply.

I decide to ignore the event and look forward to my yummy lunch.

"Hello, I'll have garlic prawns with side salad, thank you." It was not long before I sat at the table, enjoying the smell of the fresh sea air as I devour my favourite dish.

I had three skewers each with three large garlic prawns and had just eaten the last one when all of a sudden I felt extremely queer in my stomach. I was overcome with the feeling that I was about to either faint or throw up.

I grabbed my handbag in one hand and the rest of my lunch in the other and bolted for the toilet, throwing the rest of my lunch in the bin as I passed by it.

I threw open the toilet door and before I had time to think, everything that I had eaten was forcibly expelled from my mouth like a rocket, straight out. I had heard about "projectile vomiting" before but I had never experienced it myself until that moment.

If only I had listened to that voice!

My gut was never the same after that event.

A few months later I revisited Popples and talked to the café staff to find that I was not the first such case, and I reported the incident to the health authorities should further cases appear. It led to eventually having a colonoscopy and becoming gluten and dairy intolerant for many years. Although I am slowly healing, my health has never been quite the same.

Serves me right? Should I have blindly listened to the voice?

Who was it or what was it that had spoken to me in such an authoritarian voice anyway? And why was the voice so forceful? Could it be that it needed a lot of force to break through some kind of sound barrier from one dimension to another dimension? Could it be that it didn't respond to my interrogation because too much effort was involved? How do I explain this? With everything that I had been taught about life, like so many other events, I simply couldn't explain it at all. It was just another one of those incredible experiences begging to be deciphered and confirming that life is far broader than our physical existence.

This is a very difficult event to get my head around. There are obviously personalities invisible to us who can know what we are thinking and what we are about to do, yet seemingly not knowledgeable enough to understand our personality traits. I would never follow an authoritative order from a perfect stranger, let alone an invisible one! I was simply not geared to follow anything or anyone blindly.

Whatever that intelligence was, it was either not intelligent enough to know that I was not going to listen without an introduction or some kind of reasoning, or it was too difficult a task for it to break through into this dimension. The latter could certainly explain the forcefulness of the voice and the lack of response.

Throughout my life, I have heard this very same voice on four occasions, always loud and forceful and each time with excellent advice. How does that fit in with life?.

EVENT 32

333 Paramahansa Yogananda

IN MY EARLY TWENTIES, I had never taken much notice of numbers but the number twenty-two showed up repeatedly and made me take notice. If I was given a free ticket to go somewhere, it would be ticket number twenty-two, or if I was driving down an unfamiliar street looking for an address, number twenty-two would be the first number I saw.

I became increasingly aware that repetitive numbers seemed to come in waves. Each number would dominate other numbers over a period of time, and the more content and in tune I was with my life, the more this would occur. In times when I felt less peaceful and more concerned about jobs, income, survival, and general participation in hectic everyday life, the number waves would stop.

By my mid-forties, I had gone through so many waves of double and triple numbers, frequently repeating themselves, that I reached a point of wondering why these waves of numbers kept recurring and if there was any meaning in them at all.

I was going through another "three, three, three" or "triple three" stage, where triple three seemed to be everywhere. For instance, if I opened a book at a random page, it would be page three hundred and thirty-three. I ran into triple three so often that I couldn't help but take notice. I had never looked into numbers or numerology because it hadn't really taken my interest.

The wave of triple threes occurring in my life at this time was so prevalent that I decided to go to the bookshop to see if I could possibly find some kind of reference material regarding numbers.

I looked at the clock to see if I still had time to drive into to town and visit the bookstore.

The clock showed 3.33 p.m., another triple three.

I grabbed my bag and stepped into the car, which also naturally showed 3.33 p.m.

Arriving at the bookshop, I asked at the counter if they had something on recurring numbers (wondering if such a book even existed).

The bookseller led me to a section of the shop, saying that although he didn't have a book about recurring numbers or even numbers and their meanings, he did have a book that had a chapter dedicated to numbers, which might be of interest.

As we stood by the row of books that he was searching through, another book lay on a shelf on its own. It had one of those pictures of a person staring straight at you, and no matter where you stand or walk, the eyes follow you.

The book was called *Autobiography of a Yogi*. The author's name was Paramahansa Yogananda. I had never come across his name before.

I was still holding the book when my thoughts were interrupted by the bookseller. "Ah, here it is." He pulled a book off the shelf, opened it up to a back section, and showed me that there was indeed a section dedicated just to numbers.

"Thank you, I'll take that book and I would also like to take this book, *Autobiography of a Yogi*, by Paramahansa Yogananda." I purchased both books and headed off home.

It was a five kilometre drive home through the cane fields, and I had to chuckle to myself as the number plate on the car driving in front of me on the five-kilometre stretch read "333". I couldn't wait to get home to see if there was a reference in the book that might relate to the number 333.

I was very skeptical about numbers having any meaning at all but I had developed an incessant curiosity.

I arrived home and walked in with both books in hand. I placed *Autobiography of a Yogi* on the desk in front of me and searched for the number 333 in the back of the other book.

When I found the number 'three three three' and proceeded to read the meaning given; "The masters are with you and guiding you. These masters are Quin-Yan, Jesus [two or three others that I can't remember], and Paramahansa Yogananda."

"That name rings a bell," I thought as I looked down immediately to check the other book that I had bought. Yes, it was indeed Paramahansa Yogananda, complete with his picture staring straight back at me!

With so many intriguing little twists, my appetite to look deeper seemed destined to grow. I'm certain that the so-called coincidences experienced by everyone, have a greater story to tell underneath the layers of our magnificence, but why do some people seem to have more of them than others? Is it simply due to the importance one gives to them? That may certainly play a part. My own experience tells that a state of grace is also involved. In my own life experience I have without doubt come to realise that the more grateful I am for everything that comes into my life, the more these little interesting coincidences show up and the less grateful I am, the less that these occur.

Needless to say, trying to figure out how all the various facets of life fit in with each other to combine and bring together our overall functioning can at times totally overwhelm me, and it seems so complex and so wondrous and so far beyond my simple capacity to figure out, that I wish I could just go rollerblading and not think about any of it at all. But whether I have chosen this myself or not, I feel totally driven to continue unravelling the truth about ourselves, as I always have. With all these events occurring, how could I possibly not?

EVENT 33

Scrabble with Mum/Tailor

F OR THOSE OF YOU who aren't familiar with Scrabble, it is a word game where you have seven letters and out of those you need to make up a word and connect it to an existing word already placed on the board.

The seven letters that I had to play with were *O-Y-U-V-L-U-I*, and I had rearranged them on my stand to read "I luv you" and instantly thought of my boyfriend, whose last name was Tailor.

Mum was playing opposite me. Usually pretty fast at her turn, she was taking longer than usual, and my mind wandered away from the game. Influenced by my letters of play, my thoughts strayed off into the great times I had with Tailor and how I preferred to call him by his surname because I really preferred his surname over his first name.

After I spent about ten minutes on memory lane with Tailor, Mum finally moved to put down a word.

I had to have a quiet chuckle to myself as I watched my Mum place her word carefully on the board: *T-A-I-L-O-R*. Oh giggle, giggle.

This and so, so, many other similar events throughout my life, continue to confirm without question that our thinking, our thoughts, are not confined within our own physical bodies. They most certainly travel beyond our internal headspace and most certainly *do* affect others no matter how insignificant the thoughts may be. There are so many aspects to who and what we are and in at least one aspect of ourselves I believe that we all have an incredibly important role and accountability for the thought processes going on in our heads. Our thoughts affect others.

The more beautiful, and positive thoughts that we have about ourselves, the world around us, and others, the more we assist in creating a happier and healthier world. By elevating ourselves, we instantly elevate the world around us at the same time.

EVENT 34

Everything Liquefies

IN MY LATE FORTIES, I felt that I had come to understand a few aspects of life beyond the physical material body, but still many questions remained, and I was once again stretched with another totally different experience.

Since the ten-day silent meditation retreat many years earlier, when I experienced seeing microscopically inside my own body down to the single red blood cell level, I had continued practicing meditating daily. No other out-of-the-ordinary experiences accompanied those years of meditation other than the positive health benefits of sitting quietly in peace. Then one day I set my meditation timer for the usual one and a half hours and sat down to begin open-eyed meditation.

My gaze was fixed to the floor as usual, and I was concentrating on the breath entering and exiting my body when something occurred that challenged me way beyond any challenge that I had ever experienced and is really difficult to describe: the floor in front of me began to gently ripple and move, liquefy, stretch apart like chewing gum and come together again. The once solid floor was now a malleable type of stretchy liquid material, moving around, parting, spreading, and re-forming again. With each motion of stretching apart, the scene thinned to the point where it seemed to take on a see-through consistency with dark space behind it. Then it returned again to an almost solid floor, before stretching out again like a liquid wave in a new direction.

I appeared to be sitting on a solid floor that in my own new reality was actually not made of solid matter at all. Yet I was sitting perfectly still and unmoving whilst everything in the scene around me was somehow disintegrating. I couldn't grasp what was occurring before my eyes. I had never experienced anything quite like this before and my intellect is totally challenged!

I continued meditating with my eyes still fixed at the same spot, regardless of all the liquid wavelike movements of the scene surrounding me, until my alarm sounded, and my one and a half hours of meditation had come to an end. It had felt more like five minutes. Time was again to be questioned and the world was once more of solid matter. I was left numb with confusion.

From that time onwards this happened regularly, and I wondered if I had a problem with my eyesight so I decided to see what would happen if I just stared at the floor for a length of time without going into a meditative state. I found that nothing would happen no matter how long I stared at the spot, the floor remained typically of solid matter. Yet when I went into an open eyed deep meditative state, I would witness the solid matter in front of me begin to dissolve.

What was my intellect to make of this experience? As usual, I was thrown a totally new portfolio of questions.

What is going on here? Is my brain functioning properly? Could our world be an illusion?

This experience caused me to question absolutely everything. I had already discovered that we as humans are far more than we think we are but do I now have to question the very world that we think that we live in, as well?

For a long while, after I began witnessing these events, I was incredibly confused about the simplest of everyday things, like walking on a footpath, experiencing a solid world whilst also experiencing the world in a non-solid state. To say the least, it wasn't easy. And who on Earth was I going to turn to for an explanation?

The questions pervading my mind were incredibly challenging:

Am I really walking on this footpath?

Is this footpath even real?

If this footpath is not really solid, how is it that I am not falling through it?

What on Earth am I not getting here?

Is that aeroplane overhead even real?

Is that sky even real?

Is any of this even real?

Am I even real?

Am I losing the plot?

Will I end up being locked away for insanity?

I knew of no one who might have had these kinds of experiences with whom I could discuss this with, and I felt even more isolated than ever before. There were even moments when I questioned my own sanity – until I came across a set of six books called *The Life and Teaching of the Masters of the Far East*, by Baird T. Spalding.

In desperation to find answers, I purchased the set and began to scan the pages. I had only gotten through some of the first book when I realized that I was having a hard time accepting what I was reading, even though I had had so many unusual events of my own and was aware to keep an open mind. Still on the first book, I was on the verge of deciding to stop reading these books. I decided to read just a couple more chapters with as much of an open mind as possible, and if I still felt the same way, I would not continue reading any further.

The following pages shared an extraordinary event and one that I had also experienced myself. I knew if I hadn't personally experienced it, I would also have found it difficult to accept.

This gave the book enough credibility that there was truth to be found in the pages, and I continued reading the whole set, keeping an open mind.

There were many events in those books that I have personally experienced and I received great comfort from reading them. It was an even greater relief to read about an event where a group of people given accommodation in a monastery in the Himalayas all saw their room, carved out of solid rock, become liquefied and cease to be made of solid matter.

These books helped me find my own courage to write, and if I can give comfort to even just one person reading this, it is indeed worth it.

EVENT 35

Suspended inside a Bubble

I LOVED TO SIT BY the sea and meditate to the sounds and smell of the ocean, mostly during late afternoon or early evening when most beachgoers had headed home, leaving the beach deserted.

There was a small lifeguard hut with a little balcony facing out to the ocean about forty to fifty metres back from the water's edge where I would often sit, breathing in the fresh sea air, looking out over the water, and eventually go into meditation.

On this particular occasion, at a time when day meets evening, after sitting peacefully on the balcony for some time, I went into meditation, aware of the breath going in and out of my body. At this time in my life, I had been meditating regularly for approximately one and a half hours every day for some years. With eyes open, I focused on a small dint in the beach sand about halfway between where I was sitting and the water's edge.

After what seemed like twenty to thirty minutes of meditating, an extraordinary thing occurred; I found myself sitting in the centre of a giant membrane-like bubble.

Everything that I thought was "real", such as the sand below me, the ocean, the sky, and absolutely everything that I had known to be of three-dimensional, solid, material substance, no longer existed in a three-dimensional form. The world around me was now nothing more than a see-through, two-dimensional picture, rather like a movie being screened on an inside surface of a giant membrane-like bubble in which I was centrally suspended. This is so difficult to describe. It was as if everything solid had melted away from its solid state and was dissolved and then projected in a two dimensional form onto the inside of the bubble membrane, and I was mysteriously suspended, weightless, in mid-air, in its very centre.

The distance between myself, and the wall of the sphere, was about thirty metres, putting the overall size of the bubble (sphere) at some sixty metres in diameter. I was still sitting perfectly still yet somehow suspended, weightless, in the centre of the sphere and still in meditation posture.

The closest that I can come to describing the membrane is that if you were to blow up an orange-coloured balloon to its fullest capacity of air (the point just before it would explode), it would have an orange-coloured see-through quality to it, similar to what I was seeing.

So if you can, imagine that you are in a spherically perfect balloon about sixty metres across, and you are held suspended inside it, in the very centre of the space within it, with nothing supporting you, and you are looking at the inside of the *semi* see-through orange-tinted wall membrane. You see a two-dimensional picture projected on the inside of that membrane, a picture of the three-dimensional environment that you thought was solidly all around you. Instead, it is something that you are now viewing, just as you would view a movie on a screen. The membrane (sphere wall), being very thin, allows you to see through the picture which is slightly orange-tinged in colour, and you can see that the space outside that bubble is a void of what appears to be infinite black space. Nothing more can be seen other than that dark space outside the sphere, and you are all that exists inside the sphere.

Amazed at what I was looking at, I continued to sit perfectly still in my meditation position and just observed what I was looking at. This went on for what seemed a very long time, although I would guess it may have been only fifteen minutes.

I viewed this to the point where it felt that I could sit there for an eternity and never gain any understanding of what I was experiencing. I decided to close my eyes, to "close myself down" (if that makes any sense), and to get out of this situation and back to the familiar world that I thought I understood. Still, it was clear that the more I experienced, the less I understood of anything at all.

After sitting there for a while with my eyes closed, I began to become aware of the sound and smell of the ocean which had been lost throughout that experience as if the senses, other than some amount of sight, didn't exist during that experience. The inside of the sphere had been a silent void.

I opened my eyes and found myself back in the familiar three-dimensional world. I have never since had another experience of that kind.

My thoughts after this experience go immediately to the Min Min lights, spherical orbs, personalities inside "balls of light". I feel that they could well be relative to this experience. I was certainly in a sphere all my own, and although it appeared to be sixty metres in diameter from where my personality sat at its centre, I had to wonder: What if it wasn't that size at all? I recalled my meditation experience where I, or my awareness, had became small enough to see my own red blood cells, which seemed much larger than my concept of self. Had I in this instance become a personality inside an orb myself? Was that possible?

Many of the Masters of the Far East advocate that the world is an illusion. This may be a hard concept to swallow, but my own personal experiences have certainly verified that, to me, the world of solid matter is just that: an illusion. There is so much more going on. True, we can touch it, smell it, hear it, see it, and taste it. The five senses are constantly telling us that it is real. I wake up every morning into the seemingly solid "real" world and get on with my day, as we all do.

Yet I know that it isn't quite what we think it is and that it is only a small part of a far greater story.

I am convinced that thought comes before solid matter. I tend to think that thought is carried in an energy form and that it is possible that the energy or wavelengths carrying a thought can be sped up and slowed down and that it can be slowed down to the point where it has no speed at all, which is when it becomes solid matter.

My thinking process now suspects that our world is a unification of combined thought, which has been slowed down to the point where it has solidified into matter. This might also explain that if we hold an idea in our focus (our thoughts) intensely enough, then what we hold our focus upon can materialise into solid matter, resulting in serendipity, manifestations, and so on. It might also explain that if we meditate to the point of stillness where no thoughts enter our mind whatsoever, then there are no thoughts occurring to hold the world in its solidified state and therefore on some level, the world around us dissolves.

Although this may seem an amazing conclusion to come to, harnessing all of my life experiences so far, this is certainly a conclusion that my intellect can easily accept.

How incredibly fascinating!

EVENT 36

The Third Coffee Table

HAVING NOTHING BUT CLOTHES, toiletries, a few books, some personal items, and the key to a newly purchased apartment, I decided it was time to go hunting for food at the local supermarket, followed only by the task of gathering furniture to fill my empty abode with some welcome material comforts.

As I walked through a large shopping centre to buy groceries, my eye caught a set of three matching, very distinctive, exquisite coffee tables such as I had never seen before. Their aesthetic beauty stopped me in my tracks. I stood in awe of their majesty, and I was totally mesmerized.

What were they doing in this window? I was intrigued.

It was odd to see this set of coffee tables being displayed in this particular shop because the shop was a factory outlet with rows and rows of metal bed frames and piles of assorted mattresses for sale. The beautiful hand-carved coffee table set displayed in the window just didn't fit in with their sales line and were the only other pieces of furniture apart from beds or mattresses.

The price tag was a hefty five hundred and eighty-five dollars for the bigger square coffee table and two hundred and eighty-five dollars each for the two identical smaller coffee tables, making a grand total of $1,155. Ouch!

I had fallen instantly in love with them, and a coffee table was definitely on the list of furniture items that I needed to buy, so before I could count to three, my legs had placed my body right beside them. I found myself running my hands over the smooth, cool, clear resin surface protecting the middle inlaid rock and stonework set into the beautifully carved wood. On seeing the rock, my thoughts were instantly taken back into nature, walking over great boulders overlooking rivers and oceans, and I knew then that although I couldn't really afford to buy them, I just had to have them!

I approached the salesperson and tried my best to haggle, but no amount of negotiation was going to drop the price. They were far more than I could afford at the time, and when I accepted that it was not feasible financially, I asked if he would consider splitting up the set and sell me the two smaller tables.

After some heavy persuading on my part, he hesitantly agreed.

I had mixed feelings. I was relieved because the lounge room in my apartment was incredibly long and narrow and needed a long, narrow coffee table as opposed to a big square coffee table that I knew was just not going to fit at all. On the other hand I felt a real sense of guilt touched with sadness in breaking up this exquisite set.

I purchased the two smaller tables and used them as side tables. I found a long and narrow rather plain coffee table for the centre of the lounge room. Whilst living there, whenever I placed a cup on one of the smaller coffee tables, I would remember and think about that bigger coffee table that I didn't get and still felt a trifle guilty that I had split them up. Often I would think: *what a pity that I didn't get all three.*

What a shame that the big one was just too big.

If only …

I should have bought it regardless!

Oh well, I couldn't afford it anyway.

That coffee table was never going to let my mind rest! I actually missed it, even though I had never had it. I didn't regard myself as a materially minded person, and even though I never had it in the first place, I missed it!

More than a year passed, and I sold my apartment fully furnished except for my two little square coffee tables which I had enjoyed so much and couldn't bear to part with.

Every new abode that I've moved into has been a new joyful challenge in decorating. It is my favourite hobby. I see an empty home as a blank canvas on which you can create a new splash of style and colour, so I prefer to leave behind whatever I have created for someone else to enjoy. But those coffee tables were something different, and I wasn't ready to part with them. Hanging on to things wasn't like me at all, but it wasn't just the beautiful craftsmanship of the coffee tables that was special; I wasn't ready to part with how they enticed my thoughts into a natural world of jumping over boulders, dipping my feet into cool clear rivers, and hearing the gentle sounds of running water. What a joy they were!

My apartment fetched a good price, and I was ready to move into my next abode.

I found a place on the beachfront and moved in with only a few belongings, clothes, and the two small coffee tables.

It was again time to go hunting for food at the supermarket and then another search for items to furnish the new abode.

My new place had a very large square lounge room and needed a large square coffee table.

Naturally that one that got away kept jumping to mind: *If only I had bought that other big square coffee table! It would have been absolutely perfect!*

As this abode was just a rental, an in-between base whilst I looked for another property to purchase, there was no point buying nice expensive new furniture yet, so I decided to make do with whatever cheap stuff I could find for the interim period. I needed everything: fridge, bed, cupboards, rugs and everything else you need to make a home liveable and comfortable.

Driving down a main road, I noticed a second-hand furniture store and decided to check out what they had for sale.

Oh my! I think that you can probably guess what happened!

I nearly jumped out of my skin with excitement!

I just couldn't believe my eyes!

I nearly sprinted to the counter!

"How much for that large, square, carved wooden coffee table with the inlaid rocks?" I asked.

"Not sure. It only just came in today, and we only just put it out on the floor ten minutes ago. It hasn't been priced yet, but I'll go ask my boss," and the salesman disappeared through the rear swing doors.

I have to admit that I was incredibly numb with disbelief the whole time that I was waiting! What incredible timing! Or was it just that thoughts can solidify into solid matter?

Whoever had owned it (if it had been owned at all) had taken care of it, and it still looked as good as the day when I first fell in love with it.

Five minutes later, the man returned. "Two-fifty love," he said.

Two hundred, and fifty dollars! That was less than half the original new price just over a year ago!

Oh, giggle! The world is such an interesting phenomenon!

"I'll take it, thank you," I responded.

Many years have passed since then, and I still pinch myself at the memory of the journey of my three coffee tables. They certainly have their own story to tell. They moved on from my house to a friend's house while I was in between abodes and when my friends needed furniture. After a year, when they were about to sell up, the coffee tables were returned to me and back into my life again (as planned this time).

As I sit here and write, these coffee tables are just metres away, and they still continue to connect me with my beloved nature when I look at them. I think that I will be keeping them for some time yet!

Doesn't life offer some interesting moments?

What a delight!

EVENT 37

Hit by Two Trucks

IN MY LATE FORTIES, certain family events left me feeling incredibly traumatised and deeply scarred, with insurmountable feelings of hurt and incredible betrayal. I crumpled into a depression so deep that it sent me spiralling down a dark and lonely slide for the most part of ten years. I call it my darkest decade.

My usually happy-go-lucky and positive disposition had disintegrated into a depth of misery that I had never known before.

I felt such great emotional pain that it affected every aspect of my life and thwarted my ability to make the right decisions, which in turn helped continue my slide into even deeper misery.

Until my darkest decade, I had never really known just how deep and intense emotional pain could be.

I completely withdrew socially and bound my heart up with invisible barbed wire, determined not to get too close to anyone ever again. Having migrated to Australia with my immediate, rather dysfunctional family when I was just seven, I lost all of my extended loving family in one single day, and it too, had affected me greatly. I had made many acquaintances throughout my nomadic, adventurous lifestyle but resisted getting too close to anyone and relied on the safety of my own company, which I grew to thoroughly enjoy, complete with slapstick humour and dancing solo, mostly in my lounge room, to my heart's content.

I had always felt compassion for others and was ever ready to emotionally support anyone in need, but now I found myself in a desperate state of emotional collapse and needing support.

My closest friend lived thousands of kilometres away. With no network of support around me, I knew that if I was going to heal, then I would have to do it alone, without support.

I donned a big invisible mask to help me get through each day with a somewhat unconvincing smile and continued life in survival mode.

I had transformed from a happy, healthy, naive, childlike, playful, easy-going, giggling, fun-loving, and confident person into a devastated, crushed, wounded, deeply scarred, empty soul. I felt as if my spirit had been removed, as if my lovely life spark had been extinguished.

Carrying the pain of a person feeling deeply violated, I continued to function through a mask of pretence that all was well, whilst the opposite was true. I was a changed person, and I hardly recognized myself.

It was not unusual for tears to be running down my cheeks before I opened my eyes to yet another emotionally painful day, wondering if I had the strength to get myself through what I needed to conquer.

Will I ever stop crying? I wondered as I woke up each day.

I would put on my bravest heavy armour and pray that no one I was to meet that day would mention certain words that would trigger the painful memories. The word *family* was the hardest of all.

I protected myself from being in situations where those triggers might surface to open the gates to the swirling floodwaters always ready to burst out from the tumultuous ocean of tears within me.

I wore my daily mask well and became an even greater hermit than I'd ever been before.

For the first time in my life I just wasn't a happy person anymore. My life had had its ups and downs, as we all experience from time to time, but this was different. That wonderful part of me that could bounce back from any fall had completely left me, as if I had died.

With my mask fitting well, I was able to scrape through, keep my job, and earn a living, but it was a constant challenge.

All the while I hoped that one day an apology might come in the mail so that I could have closure from what had occurred and that the healing process could begin.

I could now deeply relate with the Australian indigenous people's need to hear the word *sorry* and with their need for white Australians to acknowledge openly the carnage and injustices that they had suffered and are still suffering.

For that matter, I felt that I could really empathize with anyone who had suffered any form of violation at all.

The apology that I needed in order to begin my own healing was not forthcoming, and the longer I lived in hope of that apology, the further down the spiral I slid.

"How are you?" would pierce my day regularly.

"Great, thanks," I would answer whilst the knot in my stomach tightened and the ocean inside would again be pushing against the floodgates, as I used all my energy to keep the swelling tide at bay.

Year after year, I hid behind my mask until I just couldn't take it anymore. I wanted the pain to stop. I didn't want to cry anymore. I didn't want to pretend anymore. I couldn't see myself being able to rise out of the pain, and after years of crying I didn't want to live anymore. I was exhausted, and I wanted to die.

I started wishing for a truck to hit me and take me out.

I would silently beg: *please, universe, take me. I don't want to live like this anymore. I can't stop crying, and I can't heal myself. Please, can't a truck just take me out? Please?*

And then: *crash!*

I rammed head on into a truck.

I was driving through a green light when a truck facing a red arrow decided to do a right-hand turn in front of my path. I was not able to avoid the collision.

The passenger travelling in the truck jumped out and ran over to me to see if I was OK.

"So sorry. Are you OK?" His face was red with anger and genuine concern for my welfare. He frantically continued, "I told him not to do it. I told him not to go, but he wouldn't listen!" was all I could hear as I sat in a state of shock.

I nodded that I was OK. All the while a part of me was unbelievably confused. I had been asking for a truck to take me out, and I had indeed, been hit by a truck – but why was I still here?

I felt no gratefulness to being alive at all and was quite disappointed to find myself still here.

Why didn't that truck finish me off? I was really disappointed. *I don't want to be here anymore.*

Why couldn't I have just been killed by a truck as I had asked?

Why am I still here?

Disappointed that I had to carry on with a life filled with emotional pain beyond my capacity to heal from, I went on wishing to be taken out by a truck.

After years of emotional pain still escalating to even greater heights, I was diagnosed with cancer and saw three different medical specialists. They concurred on the need to operate with urgency. I didn't believe it appropriate to save my life when I didn't feel like living anyway, so I thought that I would leave it up to the universe to decide my fate rather than the medical profession.

I didn't grow up surrounded by extended family. I was single, childless, alone and deeply wounded with little support, and now had been diagnosed with cancer. Death seemed like a blessing, but death by cancer didn't appeal at all. It was bad enough suffering emotionally, let alone having to suffer physically as well, alone in some cold hospital ward, so my wish to be taken out cleanly and quickly by a truck strengthened to new heights.

Determined not to die of cancer, I researched heavily for alternative cures. This resulted in a massive change in my diet and alkalizing my body, which seemed to manage the cancer without it spreading any further.

Soggy pillows and feelings of deep hurt continued to greet me with every new day and by now had been carved heavily into my very being. My mask was holding up nicely, and I doubt that anyone suspected the inner trauma I was dealing with.

My wish for a truck to take me out quickly continued, and I was annoyed that the first truck hadn't done the job. On my one day off per week, I decided to drive to one of my favourite rivers to spend some time in nature. I headed up the steep mountain range, winding through its endless bends.

With no "road works" warning signage having been placed on the roadside, I drove around a bend and was suddenly confronted by a line of stationary cars. I was now precariously parked just inside the white lines on a narrow road in the middle of a very tight bend.

We sat there for what seemed an eternity when a flashing police car came down from the opposite direction followed by a massively huge truck with the sign "Wide Load" across the top.

I could see that this truck was not going to be able to make the bend and that I was directly in its pathway. I could not possibly do anything to avoid the accident and time slowed right down to almost a stop, as I sat and waited for the inevitable crash.

In slow motion, my brain began the mathematics of what was about to occur. It was all very straightforward.

The roof of my car was lower than the height of the wheels of the truck and the truck would not be able to avoid hitting the rear end of my car thereby spinning the front end of my car underneath it.

Was my wish about to come true?

The first truck had failed to take me out. Was I being given another chance at that?

This truck was going to turn me into a mashed potato! Oh my God!

Crash! My body jerked from side to side, and my external driver's side reversing mirror was pushed in against my window. Strangely, all slow motion, I was now presented with a perfect reflection of my face in the mirror.

The hub of the truck's front wheels passed my window, and I can confirm that the truck was so huge and high that my car would be able to go completely underneath it. I surrendered completely without fear and was ready to depart my body.

Another jolt shook me in my seat as the truck hit the back right corner of my car, as I had predicted it would. I waited in peaceful silence to be catapulted underneath it to my predictable end.

I blanked out my mind to what was about to happen.

The truck had smashed up my car and continued on to disappear down the road.

The traffic ahead sent on up the road, and I was now sitting in my smashed up car, alone, unhurt, and very much alive.

Physics defied, how did my car not end up being catapulted under that truck? It didn't make any mathematical sense at all.

I had been wishing to be taken out by a truck, and in the same year, I had been granted crashes with two trucks, yet I was still here. Getting hit by trucks certainly wasn't delivering desired results, and being forced to look at my face in the mirror made some vague, haunting sense.

I wanted to be hit by a truck, and I got what I wanted. Twice!

Were these truck incidents just *reflecting* my thoughts the same way that the mirror was reflecting my face?

Although I was hit by two trucks, I wasn't injured or taken out. Why not?

I remembered back to the car accident that I had had in my early twenties and how I *knew* that I had a pre-set date to die and that this was the wrong date. Could it be that no matter how much I wanted to die, my pre-set date was still a long way off?

Interestingly, the last thing I saw was a *reflection* of myself looking back at myself as if confirming that somehow life is all about reflection. That like a mirror reflecting back to you, your thoughts also reflect back to you.

It seemed that I could continue being hit by trucks but that my wish to depart was not going to be granted.

Getting hit by trucks was rather uncomfortable and inconvenient to say the least, and upon realising that it was obviously not going to give me my desired result, I finally came to the understanding that I had to take on the responsibility of healing myself, regardless of whether any recognition of violation or apology ever entered my mailbox.

My darkest decade was finally showing possible signs of recovery. I had certainly learnt just how incredibly deep and intense human emotional suffering can be and how emotional pain and suffering can have a devastating effect on our physical health. I have no doubt whatsoever that it was the years of emotional pain that had caused the cancer.

The other interesting thing that I noticed as the healing process began was that during my darkest decade, other than the two trucks hitting me, I had experienced no out-of-the-ordinary events of any great significance.

Especially interesting was that once I had turned the corner – from waiting for some kind of an apology or recognition to start my healing process, to accepting that I had to heal myself regardless of anything external – it felt as if my spark had finally been lit again (although quite dimly).

The healing process had finally begun.

What a journey to endure!

For me, it was a powerful lesson of how our words and actions can greatly affect others and the responsibility we each have to be mindful of that.

I certainly believe that everything we do and everything we think affects the whole world around us and has consequences on a far greater scale than what we are mostly aware of.

For instance:

I send out thoughts that I want to be hit by a truck.

I am hit by a truck, twice.

Police are called out.

An ambulance arrives.

Three vehicles are in need of repair.

The truck owners' livelihoods are affected.

Their families are affected.

Insurance companies get involved.

Panel beaters get involved.

Et cetera. Et cetera.

And all because I had a thought!

We take our thoughts for granted as only affecting ourselves.

This is simply not the case at all.

I have learnt, many times over, that our thoughts affect the whole world around us.

Our thoughts do not simply stay within the confines of our own headspace.

Now isn't that an interesting thought?

My darkest decade also taught me that happiness does not come from outside of our selves. Rather, it comes from within our selves and is to be cultivated in abundance and shared with everyone.

EVENT 38

The Clothes Peg

M Y DARKEST DECADE FINALLY came to a halt when one morning I woke up to a dry pillow, and instead of tears in my eyes, I was captivated by the sun's golden rays filtering into my bedroom through a gap in the curtains. The room was filled with a beautiful, soft, gentle glow, and I was touched by a sense of inner peace that I had been missing for the better part of ten years.

I knew in that instant that I had crawled out of the deepest part of that dark cave that had engulfed me for so long. I could see the exit, and I knew that my healing was about to begin.

I sprang out of bed with the tingle of new hope and new life force.

Overcome with a feeling of gratefulness, I began a new day and a new life, and everything seemed different. Something had shifted.

As I showered, I could feel the water sprinkling onto my face and sensually running down my body all the way to my toes, and I thought of how lucky I was that I could just turn on a tap and step into my own private instant waterfall! I thought about all those people in third world countries who had to walk for miles every day just to get some clean drinking water, and here I was bathing in it!

Showered and ready to dress for the day, I opened my wardrobe and stood in awe to see just how many beautiful clothes I could choose from. Again, I was overcome with gratitude.

I donned a yellow dress to match the sunshine and went downstairs for a cup of tea.

I was happy, and a little recognisable piece of me had returned.

Humility flowed through my every cell as I turned on the kitchen tap to fill my kettle. I realised how easy my life was compared to most other people living on the planet. There was no fire to attend. I didn't have to watch for the water to boil. All I had to do was just push a switch at the wall, and in no time at all, the kettle would inform me that the boiling process had finished.

As I sipped my "cuppa", I looked around my lounge room, filled with big, comfortable, soft lounge chairs that were a pleasure to sink into.

I looked at all the beautiful things that I had accumulated that served no purpose other than to create an environment of aesthetic appeal for my senses.

How could I have missed all the blessings that had surrounded me every single day? How could I not have seen how fortunate I was?

With my "cuppa" finished, I loaded my washing machine and fell into appreciation all over again. Unlike so many Indian people who had to wash their clothes in the river, all I had to do was add some powder and push a few buttons. How easy could my life be?

I went out to the washing line to see if there were enough pegs. Looking up at the line, I was overcome with gratitude for the humble clothes peg.

Wow! Anyone would think that I was getting a bit carried away with this gratitude thing, but I just couldn't stop.

Standing outside, looking up at the pegs on the line, I imagined someone conceiving the idea for the first time ever to create the incredibly convenient clothes peg. I imagined that person getting pen and paper, drawing and designing the clothes peg, and then convincing a manufacturer that this would be a great thing to produce. I imagined the manufacturer pondering its viability.

And now here we all were, everyone that I have ever met in my life, from so many different continents, all using the clothes peg!

What an incredibly useful invention!

My eyes strayed beyond my washing line into the vast, infinite sky above. I had an unstoppable urge to thank whoever it was that invented the clothes peg, and with my eyes piercing high up into the sky and with total sincerity, the words of gratitude rolled out into eternity:

"Thank you, to whoever invented the clothes peg!"

It was a really good feeling to have been able to thank "whoever" for such a handy and wonderful invention, seeing that I had taken them for granted all my life. Even clothes pegs were a blessing!

I decide to check the mailbox. I walked through my carport, squeezing between my car and the side of the garden bed, and noticed an odd cone-shaped pile of leaves on my carport floor where I was just about to walk.

It was as if a whirlwind had scooped up a whole lot of leaves and piled them into a pointy little mountain. It looked odd, as there were no other leaves lying around the area. I was enticed to have a closer look at the engineering of this peculiar structure.

I was now squatting on the concrete, looking at a bunch of leaves.

After having a closer look, I noticed a speck of yellow down inside the little mountain of leaves and started brushing the leaves away.

When I had brushed the last leaves away to expose the yellow thing underneath, I was totally thrown by what I saw.

I still chuckle every time I see it!

It was a bright yellow clothes peg like no other clothes peg that I have ever seen before. It was the same size as the average clothes peg, it was unmistakably a clothes peg, but this clothes peg was in the shape of a man, complete with arms and legs, two eyes, a nose, and a very big smile on his face!

This was within seconds of my looking up at the sky and thanking whoever invented the clothes peg.

Life is indeed fascinating!

There are so many occasions like this where I am shown that the physical world around us, and our thoughts, interact. There is no question whatsoever remaining in my own understanding of that aspect in our lives. After so many experiences, my logical conclusion can only deduce that thoughts can travel within us, without us, through us and beyond us. We are constantly transmitting and receiving. And that unquestionably, at some level, the world around us, directly interacts with our thinking.

EVENT 39

Hinchinbrook Island

"**Y**OU NEED TO TAKE four days off, and don't just hang around at home," suggested my employer. "You need to go away for a real break. Let me know when you are ready, and make it soon." She was staring at me with forceful determination, underscoring that I really did need to take a break.

My mortgage sucked up my income like a vacuum cleaner high on red cordial. How on earth could I afford to go anywhere?

I gazed out of the window and into the world beyond, contemplating my choices.

Magnetic Island is only four hours' drive. Maybe I could get a small tent? That thought was immediately kicked out of my mind and replaced with *Hinchinbrook Island! That's where I want to go.*

From the first time that I had glimpsed the island from the mainland, I had wanted to explore its shores. But it was a tall request. There was no ferry, and there were no inhabitants. The island was not known for its welcoming character, being surrounded by its own natural defence system of crocodile-infested waterways and dense, mosquito-breeding mangrove forest.

But oh, once through its natural defence barriers, how captivatingly beautiful and unspoilt this island was with its stunning, towering mountains and hidden pristine beaches just beckoning to be discovered. It was a last frontier, a place hardly touched by man.

Yes! That's it! That's where I want to go!

Raising my head from my desk, I melted into my imagination and saw myself walking along its secluded pristine shores, a large pack on my back.

I felt overpowered by the force of the mountainous outcrops staring down upon me, aware of my every move. I could see myself confronted by water veins weaving their way through the forest to dissolve into the azure sea. Just magical.

I didn't know anyone who was into bushwalking, and although I was used to trekking by myself, it was not wise to undertake this particularly challenging four-day trek on one's own.

If only I had someone to go with, I wished.

As the day came to a close, I shut up shop and drove home, all the while thinking about Hinchinbrook Island.

Hinchinbrook was my last thought of the day and my first thought in the morning. I knew that going anywhere else was going to be an anticlimax. My heart was set on the impossible.

I arrived back at work to find an envelope tucked under the door addressed to me. Curious, I opened it to find a massage voucher with a note; "Please accept this as a token of gratitude for your wonderful service."

A one-hour massage would take up more time than I had to spare, but it was nice to be appreciated, and I popped it into my bag and opened the doors for business.

My thoughts alternated between my work and Hinchinbrook Island.

It was Sunday, just another working day. I worked five days for this employer but also worked Mondays at a second job for which I was scheduled to work the following day. Two and a half days had passed since my employer kindly insisted that I take a four-day break, and visions of Hinchinbrook Island kept haunting my senses.

If only I had some friends to go with! My heart yearned.

A few hours into the day, three people walked in with a question: "Excuse me, would you know the tide times for Hinchinbrook Island?"

I was stunned! I had been in this industry for at least seven years and could only recall one time when anybody ever asked me about Hinchinbrook Island; that was at least five years earlier. It wasn't even on our map as a tourist destination.

"No, sorry, I don't have any information at all on Hinchinbrook Island," I replied. Then, intrigued, I returned the question with a question: "Why do you ask?"

The ladies sat down on the couch as the gentleman explained. "We have flown up from Melbourne especially to do the four-day trek on Hinchinbrook Island and we've arranged for a water taxi to take us to the island. The boat departure time is tide related."

"How incredibly odd!" I said. "I have never met anyone who has either done that walk or even wanted to do it, and I have been sitting here for the last two days thinking of how great it would be to do that four-day trek on Hinchinbrook Island. Now in you guys walk who are about to do just that! I can't tell you how envious I am" (envious being an understatement).

The gentleman sat down on the couch next to the girls and said, "Why don't you come with us?"

This is one of those times where no dictionary on earth could come close to describing my feeling.

Did he just invite me? His words continued to echo through me. *Are these people inviting me to join them to go to Hinchinbrook? Oh God! Surely that can't be possible! I must be hearing things!*

He sat comfortably on the couch and continues his story. "We booked for a group of six, but one person had to pull out at the last minute. So we have a spot free if you want to take it. You would only have to pay a sixth share of the taxicab to Cardwell, a night's accommodation there, and your share of the return boat trip – and there's room in my tent if you don't mind sharing. You will need a backpack, mattress, sleeping bag, clothes, good walking boots, wet weather gear, food, and drinking water. We have everything else." He went on smiling at me along with the two delightful ladies sitting next to him.

I could hardly believe what was occurring.

My impossible dream was actually being offered!

I sat for a moment in stunned silence as I absorbed what was happening.

How could I ever have guessed that this might be possible?

Not only was my dream offered, but those offering were of my own age group, and I couldn't have asked for nicer people to go with!

Without a doubt I wanted in.

"When are you going?" I eagerly asked.

"We are leaving the hotel tomorrow at one," the man said.

How on earth was I going to manage this on such short notice?

I was scheduled to work for my other employer tomorrow.

There was no question that I would go. There was just how to make it happen so quickly. I didn't even have a backpack!

"Here is my mobile number. If you decide to come, call me, or just rock up at our hotel by one o'clock." He gave me his name and number, and with a friendly goodbye, off they went.

Like instant friends, I missed them already.

Sitting at my desk, totally stunned over what had just taken place, I felt a nervous tension in my stomach fuelling me into a gold medal sprint to make this come to fruition.

I immediately rang my other employer. "Hi, Angel. I have been given an incredible opportunity to do something unique tomorrow that is not likely to ever be offered again, and I would really like to have tomorrow free. I know this is short notice, but I have only just now been offered this myself."

I could hear her disappointment through the phone. Angel was a lovely person who didn't deserve to be put on the spot like this, so I tried to put her at ease;

"If you really can't do without me or find a replacement for the day, then naturally I will come to work, but I would really like to be able to take up this incredible opportunity." My fingers were crossed.

Clearly she was unprepared for my request, and I could hear the frustration in her voice as she responded. "I have to go to Cooktown tomorrow, and I can't be here to cover you. I don't know. We need to open. I just can't close the business for the day. This is very inconvenient." I could feel her concern.

"It's OK, Angel, don't worry about it. I will come to work." I really couldn't let her down, as she had always been a wonderful person and a great boss to work for.

Her voice softened. "Leave it with me and I will see what I can do."

We got off the phone and I wrote down a list of things to organise as I hadn't completely given up hope that the trip might still come to fruition.

My 'day pack' was not up to the task and I needed to buy a bigger and sturdier pack, a mattress, wet weather pants, raincoat, torch, mosquito repellent, good walking socks, and other items that one usually carries on such trips. Not to mention a visit to the supermarket to buy three meals a day for five days as well as enough water for cooking and drinking.

If it was going to happen, it would certainly be a tight call to get everything organised by one o'clock the next afternoon, but it was not impossible. Fingers and toes crossed.

I rang boss number two;

"Hi, Jolene, remember those four days off that you suggested I take?

"Yes. Where and when?" she enquired.

"Well, I know it's a bit short notice, but I have an opportunity to go with a group of people to Hinchinbrook Island for a four-day trek starting tomorrow, and I won't be back at work until Saturday. Can you manage that?"

"That's a bugger, Tilly resigned and has just left, and Inge is on holidays." She continued, "Leave it with me, and I'll get back to you."

Ring-ring. "Angel here. No worries, Viviana. My friend Tilly will look after the shop tomorrow. Have a fabulous time, and I'll see you next week."

Ring-ring.

"Hi, Jolene here. Tilly hasn't left the area yet and she is happy to come back and do your shifts for you, so have a great time, and we'll see you on Saturday then." I was ecstatic!

How very odd that both of my replacements were named Tilly and yet were not the same person! Tilly is not at all a common name, but then this whole scenario seemed incredibly odd! I had been given the green light to go ahead, and I only had to get everything done by one o'clock.

I didn't finish work till late, and I was also in the middle of making my monthly big pot of bean soup, which was a two-day process and always took a whole evening to prepare. Money was sparse, so I didn't want to waste it. I cooked late into the night before hitting the pillow, anticipating a very hectic morning and excited that I might just be able to conquer my dream.

I woke early, reread my list of necessities, and headed off to the supermarket, ready to bolt in as soon as their doors opened. I was never a natural shopper, but I managed to get everything that I needed. Then I wondered how on earth I could possibly carry all this heavy stuff on my back!

I raced home and organized meals to accommodate five days, which took longer than I had expected. Time was passing at great speed, and I hadn't phoned the others to say that I was coming because I wasn't sure if I could get everything organised in time and didn't want to hold them up.

It was now late morning, and I still had my clothes to pack and no backpack yet to pack them in, so I bundled up what I thought I needed and headed to the outdoor adventure shop in town. Time was now a serious issue.

I finally got to the outdoor adventure shop at twelve thirty, with less than half an hour to buy wet weather gear, some appropriate hiking gear, and a solid, comfortable backpack to be fitted to my body shape.

I bolted into the shop carrying all my many bags of food and bundles of clothes under my arms and blurted, "I need your help fast! I'm going to Hinchinbrook Island for the four-day trek and my ride leaves at one o'clock. We have less than half an hour to arrange a mattress, wet weather gear, all the stuff on this list, and a backpack that will take it – and all this stuff has to go in as well!" I said, dropping my bundle of clothes, food, and water to the floor.

"Twenty minutes, just twenty minutes! Can we do it?" All the while my unattended bladder was telling me that it was time, and ignoring it due to time constraints was no longer acceptable!

We had picked and fitted a sturdy, comfortable backpack, my list of purchases complete, my bladder, inconveniently, couldn't hold out any longer. "I have to use your loo. Could you start packing everything in for me as I only have a few minutes left?" I was on their loo before they even had a chance to answer. My loo activity seemed to last an eternity, but eventually I bolted back into the shop.

"Here you go then, you're all packed!" The shop assistant wryly smirked. I had only five minutes left to pay for my goods and get to the hotel!

Just as well the hotel was only a couple of blocks down the road.

I parked the car, put on my pack, and bolted into the hotel meeting area at exactly one o'clock, hoping that they hadn't left without me.

Surprised grins welcomed me as I reunited with my new-found trekking friends in readiness for Hinchinbrook Island.

I could write a whole book on the amazing and wonderful challenges that faced us on Hinchinbrook Island.

We actually endured the heaviest rain ever recorded during those four exhilarating days. Rains poured down like a waterfall from heaven.

The boat pilot had contemplated pulling out due to the prevailing winds and the increasingly choppy seas but decided to take us across as planned. It was the most adrenaline-charged boat trip that I think any of us had ever endured to say the least! I was concerned for the safety of the boat pilot on his return to the mainland after dropping us off at the island. He was indeed a brave man.

We walked for two days over mountains, crossing rivers, along ridges, down cliff faces and over rocky shores with stunning beaches and with views to delight the soul.

Then the heavens opened up with a vengeance that I had never witnessed before.

The rivers swelled and couldn't be crossed. As a local to the region, I knew that that meant salt-water crocodiles on the move.

Two days into our four-day trek we came by chance across a father and his twenty-one-year-old son who had been trekking from the opposite direction. They warned us that we needed to turn back immediately or we would not make it. The rivers couldn't be safely crossed. The man's adult son was pulled under in the raging torrent of one of the main rivers, and luckily his father, who was right next to him, managed to grab him as he was swept under.

All the walking tracks turned into creeks, and teamwork was imperative to get through without incident. Strategies were decided on. There was no way of contacting the mainland to let the boat know that we wouldn't be able to arrive at our agreed pickup point.

It was the most gruelling, challenging four days of trekking that I had ever endured. Even with wet weather gear, everything, including our feet, was wet throughout.

My backpack weighed heavily on my small physique, and as I hadn't done any overnight trekking for many years, my body ached all over.

Despite the challenging conditions, I couldn't have had a better bunch of people to journey with. Every person in the group of six was an integral part of a helpful, willing, and happy team. Despite the constant inclement weather, no one complained and incredibly, with all adversities, everyone had an amazingly wonderful time.

We were luckily able to get a ride back to the mainland with the boat arranged by the other people and radio ahead to our own pilot to let him know what was happening and that we were safe.

Our bodies had endured a tremendous amount during those four days and all I wanted to do when I got home was have a hot shower, get into dry clothes, and go and treat myself to a *massage* for my aching body.

How interesting that, on the day that I got my wish to go to Hinchinbrook Island with a bunch of instant friends, I had also received a voucher for a free one-hour massage!

It was the only free massage that I had ever been given in all the years that I was employed there. Did the universe somehow know that I would be requiring it?

How does all that work in the world of coincidences? Life is indeed full of *amazing* moments!

EVENT 40

Olive Oil!

J UST AS I HOP into my car to head home after a morning of shopping, I receive a call from my friend Trethowan to say that he had finished making my footstool and that it was ready for me to pick up.

Trethowan's place was on my way home, so I decided to pop in and pick it up immediately.

He had painted it glossy black, and it looked fabulous. After a quick chat, we popped it into my car, and I bolted home to get ready for work.

Arriving home, I brought the stool into the house and placed it in the lounge room. When I let go of the stool, I had black paint on both hands. I immediately rushed to the tap, but the water smeared it rather than washing it off. It was obviously oil-based rather than water-based paint. With no turpentine in the house to remove it, and needing to go to work with no time to spare, I was at a loss for what to do.

Amid this flurry, I recalled how a voice once tried to advise me to refrain from eating toxic prawns. As I had no better ideas, I decided to look up at the ceiling and pleadingly ask: "Universe, please, tell me what to do!"

To my absolute surprise, I got an answer! "OLIVE OIL!"

I was in awe. It was the exact same strong, domineering male voice that had warned me not to eat prawns at Popples!

How bizarre, I thought to myself. This wasn't possible, surely? But who was I to argue? I had no time to waste!

Besides the shock of getting an answer, I was also greatly amused.

I couldn't hold back a huge if hesitant chuckle, and in my disbelief, still staring at the ceiling, I gave a tongue-in-cheek reply to Mr Invisible. "Oh sure! Olive oil! Very funny!" wondering all the while how I could possibly have gotten a reply in the first place.

With nothing to lose and no better ideas of my own, I flew to the kitchen pantry, grabbed the bottle of olive oil – and to my absolute surprise, the paint wiped off like melted butter.

As I watched the paint dissolve with every wipe, question time began:

What just happened?

Whose voice was that?

How was that answer possible?

How could I hear such a loud and sure instruction and yet see nothing?

No one is going to believe me if I share this.

People will think I'm mad; after all, I am hearing voices!

Where is this voice coming from?

How many dimensions are there that we don't know anything about?

It was the exact, same, loud, authoritarian, male voice as I had experienced before, in the same tone and in the same domineering manner. That was without doubt. *So who is it? And where did it come from?*

Being female, I knew that it was definitely not my own voice or anything like my own voice.

I had a very domineering, authoritarian father, but it was not his voice either. It was not any voice that I recognized at all.

I am very aware of the general consensus that people who hear voices are mentally ill.

I certainly don't believe that I fall into that category, and each of these remarks from a voice unseen has offered excellent advice!

So *what* is that all about? How does that fit into life as we understand it?

Whose voice is it? Where does it emanate from?

There is definitely a lot more to the story of our lives.

EVENT 41

Lavender Oil!

"SOMEONE TOLD ME ONCE that it was worse than childbirth," says the radiographer as I am being prepared for a shoulder scan.

"I've never given birth, but if this is an indicator, then I'm glad I was spared the experience!" I reply in agony.

I am nearly in tears. I have never experienced physical pain quite like this before. It makes a toothache seem like a gentle caress.

The injury was brought on by a fall down a steep embankment where I had landed hard on my shoulder.

I had ripped the tendons, and the pain was excruciating. My arm in a sling to minimize movement, I couldn't dress myself, and I had to sleep sitting up as it was too painful to lie flat. I couldn't drive, I was totally dependent on someone else to carry out the simplest of tasks, and coping with the constant pain was exhausting.

The radiographer finished scanning, and from there we went to the medical centre.

Apart from ripped tendons, I had calcification of the bone, and my x-ray showed that I had spurs, which are hard calcium deposits growing out from the bone. The two problems together exacerbated the pain.

"You've got rotator cuff calcification tendonitis, and it's going to take at least six months to heal. You'll need regular cortisone injections just to manage the pain over the next six months." The doctor's words came slowly as he continued to look at the scan on his computer. Finally he turned to the prescription pad and pen which lay next to him on the desk.

Having read some terrible things about the side effects of cortisone, I really didn't want any of that going into my body.

"I don't like the thought of six months on cortisone. Is there something else that can help me, with fewer side effects?" I asked.

"It's the only one that's going to do anything for you," he insisted.

"Well, thank you, but I prefer to manage without it."

He looked at the time, and we nodded to acknowledge that our fifteen minutes had come to an end. As I pulled the door open to depart, the doctor turned to me and grimly muttered, "Terribly painful, next six months."

My friend drove me home very carefully, as even the slightest change in the road surface ripped painfully through my shoulder. I thought in silence, *How am I going to cope with this constant, excruciating pain?*

We had only been driving for five minutes out of town when I couldn't bear it anymore. In desperation I closed my eyes and turned to the universe for advice and in my silent suffering asked, *Universe, please, I cannot bear this pain. Please tell me what to do.*

"GET LAVENDER OIL!"

I was totally blown away! I really hadn't expected an answer!

I looked at my friend, stunned, and wondering if he had heard that voice too.

He obviously hadn't heard what I had just heard, loud and clear, resonating from the space that enveloped us both yet, only I heard it.

There was no mistaking that it was the very same authoritarian, domineering male voice that had assisted me a couple of times before.

I had no idea what my friend's reaction would be, but I needed to share what I had just experienced. "You are not going to believe this, but I just asked the universe what to do, and it answered me with '*Get lavender oil!*'"

He turned to look at me, and I felt that he totally believed me.

I didn't say another word, and when we got to the next exit, without my asking, he turned the car around and said that we might be able to buy some at the market.

"Do you have any 100 per cent pure lavender oil?" we asked the appropriate stall keeper.

"Yes, I most certainly do," she said, passing us a small bottle.

"Would you have a bigger one? Or better still, what is the biggest one that you have?" I enquired.

"This is the biggest," she said, handing it to me.

"Thanks, I'll take it, and no need to wrap it," I explained as my friend pulled out my purse and handed her the money.

I couldn't wait to try it to see if the "voice unseen" was once again giving me good advice, and I applied some immediately,

Within minutes, it seemed to soothe the area. I wondered if it was just the calming nature of lavender oil's scent that was calming or if it was indeed having some immediate effect.

I put the lavender oil on regularly, day and night, and the pain eased.

Within two weeks I was completely healed, functioning, and totally back to normal.

"Six months of cortisone injections!" I was so glad that I hadn't taken the doctor's advice. I thanked the universe.

Many months after my healing, I opened the bathroom cupboard where I had placed the bottle of lavender oil and I tried to shift the bottle but couldn't move it.

I tried again, lifting the bottle with a bit more force and as it finally lifted off the shelf, I was amazed to see that it had dissolved the white paint where it had been sitting, exposing a ring of wood underneath.

Now that makes a lot of sense, I thought. *If lavender oil can dissolve hardened paint, then it can be absorbed through the skin and dissolve the calcium build-up growing from the bone.*

I still believe that that is how I healed so quickly but *who was it that knew that?* I asked myself.

Again I was left with many unanswered questions.

Why did I get the answer this time? Why so many times in my life do I plead for answers and don't get any response at all?

How does this all work and fit together?

Who or what is it that chooses what to respond to?

There is definitely more going on here, but why can't I get what that voice is?

Whose voice is that?

Where is it coming from?

By this stage of my life, this very same voice had advised me well on four occasions, each separated by many years.

The voice was loud, clear, strong, authoritarian, and male. On each occasion the voice seemed omnipresent, resonating from both the space outside me and the space inside and through me.

On three of these occasions I was totally alone, but on one occasion I was in a car with a friend who did not hear the voice even though, to me, it seemed to permeate the whole space in the car.

These four events have left me questioning what really happens with people who suffer schizophrenia and hear voices.

Is it possible that the voices they hear, at least some of the time, are actual, real personalities taking over a part of their physical existence?

I remember when I held a marketing manager position for a large company many years earlier when a gentleman, who had not made an appointment, had walked straight into my office wanting to urgently speak with me.

He was well presented, dressed in suit and tie, carrying a briefcase, well spoken, and seemingly gentle in nature.

I decided to give him that time and invited him to sit down.

Within minutes and before I could grasp the reason why he needed so urgently to speak with me, his whole demeanour changed. He was no longer well spoken, his posture became sluggish, and he started a completely different conversation that had nothing to do with what he was previously talking about. In addition, there was an aggressiveness that wasn't there before.

I felt that I was now confronted by a totally different personality.

I was still struggling to grasp the gentleman's reason for coming to my office when he again changed his posture and started to cry. His voice changed, and I was now faced with a person who was obviously totally distraught and unable to convey what he was saying through his incessant crying.

In the meantime I was trying to make sense of what was happening in front of my eyes as I had never witnessed anything like this before. I felt totally inadequate when it came to what to do and how to handle the situation.

After a couple of minutes, the crying ceased, and he sat upright in his chair and continued the initial conversation as the gentle, well presented, well-spoken man who had first walked into my office.

He had obviously no recollection of what had taken place in between. Not even his incessant crying, which had me truly amazed.

After a few minutes as person number one, he again turned into person number two, and once more his posture changed. The politeness in his voice disappeared, and the sluggishness in his posture returned but this time with some rather frightening aggressiveness: he got up from the chair and towered over my desk. I felt very threatened by his behaviour, but all the while, I was careful to stay very calm, wondering how to deal with what was going on.

Just as I was most concerned for my safety, person number three appeared, and he fell back into his chair and burst into another heavy bout of loud crying.

I felt incredible compassion for this man who was obviously three totally different personalities in the one body, yet not one of these personalities seemed to have any awareness of the others even existing.

Whilst he was sitting there crying loudly for the second time, I took my chance to get out of the office as quickly as possible for my own safety.

"I'll be right back, I'm just going to get you a box of tissues," I said and left the man alone in my office.

I immediately went into the neighbouring office of a male colleague and explained what was happening. He immediately rang the desk of another male colleague and asked him to come to his office; there would be two people for safety reasons. He then accompanied me to my office along with the box of tissues.

"Hello, this is Mr. Jenson who may be better able to assist you." After I introduced them, Mr. Jenson kindly escorted the man out of my office to his own office where the other colleague was waiting to assist. As for the box of tissues, my visitor had in the meantime become person number one and would have had no memory or connection to the box of tissues that I had gone to get him, so I handed the box to my colleague.

Recollecting that experience in my office and reflecting on my own earlier experiences where the personality of an aboriginal boy joined me in my body to run over the rocks and thirty years later, my father's personality joins me in my body to dance in the gallery, the difference here is that I was totally aware of the dual personalities sharing my body at the same time, whereas in my visitor's case that awareness wasn't there. That was an interesting observation.

Also having been given advice by a very clear, bodiless, male voice on four separate occasions throughout my life, I have to wonder whether people suffering from schizophrenia are being misdiagnosed as having a mental illness, when it may be something completely different.

EVENT 42

Mrs Priestly

M Y BEST FRIEND IN high school lived on a dairy farm, and I always enjoyed spending time there with her and her rather large family. Her mum always welcomed me with open arms and treated me as if I was just another one of the bunch.

Sometimes, if I felt down, I would reminisce about those happy farm days, and the memory alone proved to be an effective pick-me-up. I had wonderful recollections of playing duets on the farmhouse piano, riding horses, getting on the tractor to round up the cows – even the smell of silage was all it took to put a smile on my face again.

Those were some of the most endearing memories of my life as an adolescent in Australia, and for those times, I feel blessed and I am forever grateful.

I left home at the age of fifteen, moving from Victoria to Sydney. There I found work and got on with my independent life. I caught up with my best friend only on a couple of occasions throughout the following ten years, and after that, all contact was finally lost.

Thoughts of those days had faded over the next thirty or more years, eventually disappearing into some buried archive in the extensive filing cabinet of my mind.

Yes. Thoughts of those days had long past.

I opened the cutlery drawer to get out a spoon when all of a sudden an image of my old school friend jumped into my mind. It took me completely by surprise, and my immediate thought was *Oh wow, Penny! I wonder how she is doing. I wonder what she is doing with her life. I wonder how her mum is.*

I then stopped. With a touch of sadness, I realized that her mother would be quite old by now and possibly even not alive anymore.

I also wondered why now, after all those years, they would suddenly pop so crisply and clearly into my mind!

I quietly hoped that they were all well and having good lives. Then I went on with my day and my own life.

Two days later my phone rings and I answer;

"Hello, Viviana here."

"Is that Viv?" the caller asks.

I recognise the sound of the voice immediately but don't have a clue who it belongs to other than that it's someone from a very long time ago as no one has called me "Viv" since my teens.

"Penny's mother here," says the familiar voice. "I'm having my ninetieth birthday party and I would love you to come."

It was wonderful to hear Mrs Priestly's voice again and know that she was still very much alive!

This is such a common occurrence. Has anyone ever *not* had a situation like this? I think that it would indeed be hard to find someone who hasn't.

I simply concluded that when they were mulling over the guest list two days earlier, discussing me as a possible guest, the receiver of my mind simply picked up the signal that they were omitting. I have understood from a very young age that we are all transmitters and receivers, whether we know it or not, and I am constantly reconfirmed that all of our thoughts carry out beyond our own physical headspace. This is just another example of so many.

Often when I have shared my ideas with people, they have responded with "What a great idea, you should patent that."

I have never really felt 100% certain that our ideas are our own great ideas. Although, they may well feel like it. The thought has certainly struck me that it is possible that an idea already existed and that my receiver simply picked up the frequency that carried the information.

Whether that is true or not, from everything that I have experienced, I can only logically deduce that we all share our thoughts and are subjected to those of others, collectively, beyond our physical nature.

And in being so, would it not be imperative that we, each single individual person, *must* find our hearts and fill the world with loving thoughts, regardless of what adversities we have to face, if we genuinely want to live collectively in a nicer world?

I have constantly been shown through my many experiences that our thoughts are not confined to the limits of our own physical boundaries.

I have without doubt come to believe that every thought that you have goes out into the bigger cosmos, the bigger brain of which we are all an integral part and I believe that we are all taking part in this amazing phenomena regardless of our awareness of it. I have been shown over and over again that we are so much more than we think we are and that there is so much more happening around us than we seem to be aware of.

EVENT 43

Merrilly

KEEPING IN CONTACT WITH people was never a great talent of mine. I always felt that once a person was in your heart, they were always a part of you regardless of distance, so communication wasn't really imperative to long distance relationships.

After moving thousands of kilometres north from the southern state of Victoria to the northern state of Queensland, my contact with people that I used to hang out with in Melbourne dissipated, and I got on with my new life in the tropics. After many years, most of those contacts were usually lost altogether.

Occasionally something would come up in my life calling for a brief return to Victoria. I had one particular friend whom I would always ring up whenever I found myself in the heart of the city of Melbourne where she worked. Even though we never communicated throughout the years in between my visits, we always enjoyed catching up over either a cup of coffee or lunch, depending on the time of day.

I always felt a strong connection with her, and whenever we met, we just picked up from where we left off many years before, as if no time had elapsed since our last coffee together.

I had just touched down in Melbourne, and Merrilly was having a day off work. We spent a wonderful afternoon together, hanging out at her place, chatting away in the sunroom and just enjoying each other's company. Before we knew it, the evening was upon us, and we adjourned to the kitchen.

Merrilly loved cooking. No matter what she prepared, it always melted in my mouth in such an orgasmic way that it felt like a crime to swallow.

"I still can't believe that you don't like cooking." She cheekily stared at me to see if I had any signs of maturing in the kitchen whilst continuing to madly chop a handful of garlic as if she was born doing it.

I stayed the night, and the following day we enjoyed a long walk through nearby parklands, after which we parted ways, knowing, as usual, it would be years before we would catch up again.

I always found it interesting that when I was back in Queensland, thoughts of Merrilly never entered my mind, and yet I could never touch down in Melbourne without thinking of her instantly.

Years had gone by since my last visit to Melbourne, and I was just living my life in Queensland when Merrilly's face, looking straight at me, flashed before my mind's eye. I wondered how she was and thought maybe I should call her.

I didn't call.

During that week Merrilly popped into my mind three times. Each time I was tempted to call but didn't.

I wonder why Merrilly keeps popping into my mind. Maybe I should just call her, I thought. I didn't call.

A few days later, my phone rang, "Hello, Viviana here."

"Hello, Viviana, it's Merrilly's boyfriend, Hamish, here. I'm sorry to inform you that Merrilly unexpectedly passed away after a week in hospital suffering from a blood clot in her brain. I'm terribly sorry."

Merrilly and I often talked about life after death, and I have no doubt that she would have thought of our conversations whilst lying in her hospital bed. I suspect that every time she did so, I was picking up her thoughts.

So how do we know when we are being thought of?

When we think certain things, the relevant areas of our physical brain are activated, and as we learn more, we continue to develop that intricate network of highways that connect information in our brains.

I have come to believe that on one level of our multi faceted existence, at this stage of my own journey, from everything that I have so far experienced, that as in the physical brain, we also have what I am going to call our *Unified Cosmic Brain*. I believe that in our *Unified Cosmic Brain* we also build frequency or vibrational highways that interconnect all of us. In this way the information we carry and everything that we do and think on the physical level is building the interconnecting pathways of our bigger, interconnected, single *Unified Cosmic Brain*.

So when we become very close to someone, we build a stronger highway in the *Unified Cosmic Brain* that builds a type of frequency speedway connecting us directly with that particular person. I believe that we all have that ability available to us but that we need to discover how to fine tune ourselves for better reception. This may mean clearing our minds of unnecessary activity in order to be more freely receptive. I suspect that the more that is going on in our minds, the more interference there will be. Spending time in silence or silent meditation may assist in clearing the way for better receptivity. How exactly we receive and transmit is still a mystery to me, but that we do, leaves not one iota of doubt whatsoever.

EVENT 44

Mum Passes Over and Spends Time with Me

I T WASN'T UNTIL VERY late in our lives that my mother and I finally managed to build a real, honest, and loving relationship.

My immediate family, in my own evaluation, had been greatly dysfunctional. I had left my immediate family many times, only to return each time with the hope that "this time it may be better," but the same old patterns full of drama would repeat, and I would depart again for the sake of a more peaceful existence.

Love and affection had never been a part of growing up in any of the relationships within our immediate family of five. In my late forties I was tired of the lack of progress and poor attitudes that continued to squash any hope of creating an honest, warm and loving family environment.

My father had already passed away many years before, and the opportunity of building any kind of joyful relationship, or closeness, with him, was already long gone. My only prospect of ever experiencing a totally honest, and truly genuine and loving family relationship was with my mother, and it was well overdue. It was now or never.

At this stage in my life, I had not ever heard the words *I love you* from either parent – not to me, not to each other, not to my other siblings – I had never witnessed any sign of affection between my parents and I was now in my late forties. My parents' relationship, in my eyes, was a complete disaster. We had been five human beings putting up with each other because we had to, and it was an ugly way to grow up. I loved my mother, and I suspected that her indifference was a mask that she wore well in order to hide her own feelings of hurt and disappointment, a skill that had been passed on to me as well.

It was time for change. It was *definitely* time for change! Otherwise I was ready to give up and walk away forever.

I plucked up the courage to ask a very difficult question: "Mum, do you love me?"

She shrugged as if to give it a bit of thought and replied, "No, not really."

"Well then, Mum, do you like me?" I asked.

"No, not really," she replied.

Her answer didn't surprise me at all, as love and affection had never been part of our family lives.

"Well, I'll tell you what, Mum," I said, deciding to give her my ultimatum. "See my car over there in the driveway?"

Mum looked over towards my car.

"I'm going for a walk around the block, and whilst I'm away, you will have time to think about whether or not you want to build a loving relationship with me." I continued, "That means that you will have to start finding reasons to like me and" – in a very clear and determined voice – "make a genuine decision to begin to love me.

And when I come back from my walk, I will ask you if you want to build that loving relationship, and if your answer is no, I will hop into that car and drive down that driveway, and you will never see me again."

My mother instinctively knew that I meant every word that I was saying with a determination not to be taken for granted. We stared into each other's eyes for a moment, and I added, "I suggest that you have a really good think about that." Then I headed off on my walk around the block.

I was away for about twenty minutes and returned to see my mother sitting in the garden in the backyard, and I proceeded to sit beside her.

"Well, Mum, what decision did you come to?" I asked.

"You don't have to go," she said.

"That's not what I'm asking, mum," I replied.

A deafening silence followed for some minutes.

I knew that this was a very difficult and crucial moment in our lives, but it was necessary. It had to be her decision to make.

I broke the silence with "I shall go and make us a cup of tea, and after that I shall start to pack my bag."

I brought out a cup of tea, and we sat together sipping silently.

I eventually finished my tea and broke the silence: "Well then, Mum, I guess it must be time for me to gather my belongings," and I got up off the seat in readiness to go.

"OK," she said.

I wasn't going to let her get away with such a pathetic answer, as I was looking for real commitment and certainty. "OK what, mum?" I asked.

She knew me well enough to know that this was a serious moment! "OK, I will do everything that I possibly can to see that we build a happy, loving relationship," she answered, looking straight into my eyes. I knew that she realised what was happening, and I knew that she had wholeheartedly made that choice.

From that moment on, my mother and I became great friends.

We found many things in common. We danced in the lounge room, chuckled through the walls of our bedrooms at night, played backgammon, scrabble, and cards, and on cold mornings we would even hop into each other's bed and chat the morning away, which we had never ever done before.

Mum was getting old, and I had moved into my mother's house. It was one of the most wonderful times of my life, and I can confidently say that it was also one of her happiest times too. We continued to build our relationship and lived and shared like friends sharing a house together, having fun, splitting all the bills and responsibilities, and feeling a great sense of satisfaction that we were able to conquer what once seemed impossible. We had united in our ability to conquer the past and formed an honest and loving relationship.

Through disturbing family circumstances outside of our control, I had to depart my mother's side and was unable to have safe and comfortable access to her. We had been ripped apart, and I missed her terribly throughout the last decade of her life. I have no doubt at all that she missed me as much as I missed her. We had formed a very close bond. I entered what I refer to as my darkest decade. I felt terribly robbed of the happy and loving relationship that we had both been dedicated in building, and when she passed away a decade later, it was for me as if my mother had died twice.

My siblings had not contacted me to say that my mother had had a stroke and was on life support. She had been on life support for five hours before an extended family member had kindly contacted me. I flew down to Victoria as soon as I could to sit by her bedside and hold her hand, but my siblings had decided to take her off life support before my arrival.

I felt too unsafe to attend my mother's funeral, and I made the very difficult and heart-wrenching decision, not to attend. Instead I returned to Queensland.

It was a really hard week to endure. I loved my mother.

My favourite clock had been broken for many years. It was a small round clock housed in a funky gold exterior casing that stood on three curly legs. I had tried to find a replacement for the removable centre clock piece but to no avail. I couldn't get myself to throw it out. It had been a gift from a friend, and it never ceased to put a smile on my face each time I saw it. So for many years, it was nothing more than a much-loved, non-functional ornament.

A week had passed since my mother had died. I drove down the road to go to the post office and had an incredible feeling that my mother was with me, accompanied by a strong urge to stop the car.

I stopped the car and sat in a moment of silence as I felt my mother's personality sitting next to me in the passenger seat of my car. It was a wonderful feeling of reunion.

You're just imagining things because you miss her, I told myself. I peered out the car window, and my gaze fell directly upon a local op-shop in the distance. I felt a strong urge to go and have a look inside.

"Oh wow!" I said to the lady behind the counter. "I've searched for one of these for years!"

It was a rectangular frame, covered with painted butterflies and had the same centre clock piece as my funky round clock at home.

I took it straight to the counter to make the purchase and the attendant told me, "I've been looking at that frame all morning. It's beautiful, and I love the butterflies and would have bought it myself if it was a frame, but I don't need a clock."

"Oh, I can fix that," I responded as I pushed the clock out of its frame and passed her the frame. "You can have it. I only need the clock part" and I paid her the one-dollar price.

Driving home, I remembered how so many cards that I received from my mother had butterflies on them. She loved flowers and butterflies, but I didn't think much more about it.

I was excited when I got home to discover that the clock was a perfect fit in the casing of my funky gold clock as I expected it would be and that it worked perfectly.

The following day I drove down the mountain range to do some shopping in the next biggest shopping hub from where I lived. I had three things in mind to buy: an out-dated Trivial Pursuit game that was no longer produced, tea towels, and an identical replacement handbag.

On my way down the mountain I was overcome with joy as suddenly, halfway down the range, I could feel my mother's presence watching over me from an area above the front of the car, as if she was looking over me through the windscreen.

I looked up at the sky and very loudly said, "Hi, Mum, I can feel you! I can feel you." I felt my mother's presence accompany me all the way down the mountain and all through my shopping spree. I could feel she was with me, and just as we had done in the past, she was shopping with me again, only this time I couldn't see her, but I could unmistakably *feel* her.

"Mum, I need a game of Trivial Pursuit. Let's see if there is one in the second-hand store." I walked in and headed for the section where games can be seen.

"Oh, yes! Thank you!" The *very top* board game on the pile was indeed Trivial Pursuit. I was incredibly impressed.

I loved my handbag, but it had started to wear out, and I needed to replace it. I had met a lady at a group gathering who commented that she loved my handbag and wondered if it might suit her needs too. It was an expensive bag, so I explained that I was about to buy myself another one, and if she wanted my old one to try it out first, she was welcome to it. She was really grateful for my offer, and that was the plan.

I dropped the Trivial Pursuit game off at the car and headed for the handbag shop, feeling my mother's presence with me the whole time. I walked into the shop and found that they had the exact replacement bag that I was looking for – which was no great surprise, as that was where I had purchased it in the first place.

Walking out with both my old and my new handbag, I now entered the department store and quietly asked, "OK, Mum, lead me to the tea towels." I was led straight to the tea towels without having to enquire as to where they might be.

"Thanks, Mum. Now I have a really, really, really, really, big ask," I silently told her and explained: "I met a lady, and I have no idea where she lives, and I want to give her my old handbag. Can you present her for me?"

Having only just gotten the tea towels and asked the question, I turned the corner of the next aisle, and we almost collided! Wow! Needless to say, it was indeed an electric moment! I was able to hand over my old handbag!

"Thank you, mum!"

My mother's presence stayed with me for six weeks after her passing, and many wonderful and interesting events occurred during that time. (I could write a book on that alone). Then one day when I was standing in the middle of my lounge room, next to my couch, I felt the very instant that her presence departed. It was a powerful moment, and I knew without any doubt whatsoever that she would not return. I often wonder whether her personality moved into another dimension or whether her personality had taken on a new body for a new human experience. I have no idea and can only speculate what might have occurred. I can only speak from the events that I have personally experienced and I am sure that there is so much more waiting to be discovered. I am confident that I have only just slightly scratched the surface of magnificence beyond my comprehension.

IN CONCLUSION

NOW IN MY EARLY sixties, with everything that I have witnessed and experienced, along with my intuitive feelings and intellect, I have assembled all the pieces of the jigsaw puzzle of my life together. I have now come to the understanding that we are incredible, multifaceted, unique beings who function on many levels. We have not only a physical form, we are also formed of energy. We are transmitters and receivers, constantly sending and receiving information that travels through matter, time, and space, and all our thoughts combine to affect each other.

We are all equally important and unique, with the capacity to merge with each other as one. Our personality does not fill the entire space of our body, and it is possible for the body to house more than one personality at the same time (as I experienced in the events with the aboriginal boy and also with my father).

We have the ability to visually see down to the molecular structure inside our physical body without any external aid of a microscope.

We can sense, hear, and feel other invisible personalities even though our visual spectrum is not yet equipped to see them.

We are not alone in this realm that we inhabit, and there is much more going on than our five bodily senses are capable of picking up.

Our lives can be intercepted from a place beyond our vision and understanding.

Death only touches the physical body; our personality continues beyond.

Our lives are on some level recorded, and we are accountable for our actions.

Departure from the physical body may well be predetermined.

Time is not what we perceive it to be. Time can bend, overlap, stretch, and shrink. Time can be divided to split a given event into both kinetic and motionless states simultaneously.

We are able to have factual knowledge of, and visually see, the future, before it arrives. Past, present and future at some level, already pre-exists and involves time, which is malleable.

And ultimately, I have seen the great illusion: that the material world we see is not solid and that we only perceive it to be real.

All of these experiences have led me to decipher that, just as the neurons in our brains are constantly sending information and signals from one to another without physically touching, on a much larger scale, each one of us is also constantly sending out and receiving individual thoughts, information, and signals without physically touching.

My experiences have shown me that our own private thoughts are not confined to our own individual headspace. Instead they emanate out and beyond us, as if we are all neurons in one giant cosmic brain. In the unison of combined thought, together, we create and solidify or "hold" collectively the physical world that we are experiencing and living in.

Simply put, we are all together one rather amazing phenomenon. We are creating our life here on this level in such a way that we thoroughly believe that we are totally separate from each other, when actually, we are not. We are all in the illusion together, manifesting the world as we believe it to be.

I have no doubt that I have just scratched the surface of something way beyond my capacity to understand at this time and that there may be infinite dimensions.

My conclusion is that on one level of our multifaceted lives, we all have an important, equal share in creating the world that we are experiencing, and therefore we all have an equal responsibility and ability to affect it.

We are co-creators. We affect each other and we are in this together. We are all connected and in unison creating the world that surrounds us.

It is not an easy task to drop the thick layer of conditioning that we have all been subjected to throughout our lives. We have responded to our conditioning by building barriers: we judge, criticize, label, isolate and group.

I believe that it is in our nature to want to gather information, to feed our brains in order to grow, expand and create. If you want to become an engineer, a sculptor, or a mathematician or to specialize in anything, then you must gather the information and experience to feed the brain into developing in that direction and focus on the goal in order to bring that lifestyle to fruition.

I believe that on a much larger scale, it is no different with our single greater *Unified Cosmic Brain* of thought waves creating the world that we want to experience.

We co-create our world lifestyle by the information, thoughts, and signals that we individually give to it. Our world is "held" in its solid physical form by the collection of our unified thoughts and beliefs and then seemingly verified through our so-called "senses" so that we believe the physical aspect to be real.

Since it is our nature to want to grow and expand ourselves, we are drawn to watch programs like the news, which unfortunately concentrates its efforts on reporting the negative tragedies happening around the world rather than the positive, therefore giving the impression that we live in a rather depressing world. We then absorb that thinking and start to believe that it is so. Those beliefs then become united, to co-create and develop the greater, cosmic brain, and together we manifest "as one" a world that reflects back to us in response to our thinking and beliefs. We need to focus on the positive if we wish to develop a positive world.

I am no guru, spiritual master, psychic, or scientist. I am not adherent to any belief or religion, and I belong to no label. Although I have experienced many events, I cannot make them happen at will. I have just seen glimpses of a bigger picture. I am nothing more than another part of the amazing phenomenon we call the universe, of which we are all an equal and integral part and in which we are all intimately connected.

I believe that we are all capable of developing the ability to experience the "more" that is available to us, which is obscured by both our conditioning and the business of our hectic daily schedules.

I know that we are much more than we think we are and that we equally have a tremendous capacity to do great and wonderful things for the greater happiness of all beings.

When we look into the eyes of a baby smiling back at us, it is easy to fall in love. I believe that what we are really seeing in that instant is our true self and the recognition of what and who we are deep beneath our conditioning: for a moment we subconsciously acknowledge the underlying truth of that pure essence that we are, as it shines through the baby, who has not yet been subjected to a life of conditioning.

I also believe that we all play an integral part in manifesting our overall individual journeys in this physical aspect of our existence, and I hope that sharing my journey with you enables you to see how important you are in the greater scheme of things.

I can certainly conclude that you are far greater than you might think you are. You affect the world and everything in it.

We may feel alone and separate in our physical human state, but that is only one small part of a far greater and more glorious experience of which every one of us, including you, is an important and inseparable part.

May the sharing of my life journey assist you in your own journey and help you see that your own conditioning is not what you truly are. Nor for that matter is anyone else's. May you find your true self beneath it, and in discovering your true essence, may you cultivate that joy and share it with everyone.

—Viviana Verheesen

A BRIEF SUMMARY

Event 1. The Mystery Begins.

   -We are transmitters and receivers.

Event 2. An Invisible Playmate.

   -Personalities, beyond our range of vision, exist.

   -The personality does not fill up our whole body entirely.

Event 3. Saved by the Same Stranger, Twice.

   -Our lives can be intercepted from a different dimension.

Event 4. I Died on the Wrong Day.

   -Pre-set date for departing the physical body.

   -There is no death.

   -Our life is recorded, and we are accountable.

Event 5. The Haunted House and the Beautiful Being of Light.

   -We are multidimensional beings.

   -We are physical matter.

   -We are radio frequency.

-We are light frequency.

-We are energy bodies.

-We are personalities.

Event 6. Time Splits.

-Motivated and unmotivated time coexist.

-Personality can shift in and out of the physical body.

Event 7. An Out-of-Body Experience.

-Personality can move through matter.

-We wear our bodies like we wear a garment.

Event 8. The Box of Photos.

-Our thoughts travel beyond our selves.

-Our thoughts affect others.

Event 9. Acknowledgement of a Future Time.

-Factual acknowledgement of a future time.

-Are we pre-programmed?

-Information is carried via wavelengths.

-Past, present and future already exist.

-Time is questionable

Event 10. The Buttoned-Up Jacket.

-External guidance.

-Thoughts become things.

Event 11. A Surprise Visitor in My Gallery.

-Father takes control of my body.

-Two personalities in one body.

-Deceased personalities are still very much alive.

Event 12. I Know Everyone Intimately.

-We are one phenomenon

-We know each other intimately

Event 13. Being Watched as I Move into My Apartment.

-Humans are capable of incredible sensitivity.

-Sensing events occurring from a great distance away.

-We are all linked.

-We are like neurons in a larger cosmic brain.

Event 14. Blue Energy Rises from My Body.

-We have a light body.

-We have an energy form that is separate from the physical form.

Event 15. Red Blood Cells.

-We can see microscopically inside our physical bodies.

-Our vision is not confined to our physical body.

Event 16. A Foreigner on a Pushbike.

-Coincidences and synchronicities.

-The universe has a sense of humour.

Event 17. The Ford Transit Van.

-Manifestation.

Event 18. The Bending of Time.

-Time is malleable.

-Time can freeze, split, stretch, and shrink.

Event 19. The Paper Clip Man.

-Our thoughts can be intercepted.

-We can be guided from a dimension beyond our awareness.

Event 20. The Pencil Appears.

-Manifestation.

Event 21. Our Thoughts Affect Others.

-In partnership, together, we create the physical world.

-Each thought that we have affects everyone as a whole.

Event 22. Min Min Lights?

-There are many dimensional aspects to human life.

-Personality is separate from the physical body.

Event 23. I'm Now in the Future.

-Precognition.

-The moving picture of life.

Event 24. Wonderful Serendipity.

-Living with Gratitude.

Event 25. Need Signature Now.

-There is more going on than we dare to believe.

-We need to shed our conditioning to expose the truth.

Event 26. Hot Air Balloon.

-Precognitive dreaming.

-Consciousness continues to work whilst the physical body sleeps.

Event 27. Pennies from Heaven.

- Does a cosmic centre of control decide what we are given?

- Denial being used to ease the discomfort of mystery.

Event 28. A Tiny Little Kombi Van.

-The universe has a sense of humour.

-Where do the gifts come from?

Event 29. Fate.

-Free choice.

-Evolution.

Event 30. Mum Falls into the Gutter.

-Unalterable preordained events.

-Is the future really in our own hands?

Event 31. Prawns at Popples.

-An invisible voice warns me for the sake of my wellbeing.

-Inter-dimensional sound barrier

Event 32. 333 Paramahansa Yogananda

-A state of Grace.

Event 33. Scrabble with Mum/Tailor

-Thoughts are beyond our headspace.

-Elevating our thoughts elevates the entire world.

Event 34. Everything Liquefies.

-Could solid matter be the greatest illusion of all?

Event 35. Suspended inside a Bubble.

-Thoughts slow down to solidify into solid matter.

-Unified thought creates our world, which is seemingly verified through our senses.

Event 36. The Third Coffee Table.

-Whatever we focus upon can mysteriously be presented.

Event 37. Hit by Two Trucks.

-Be careful what you wish for.

-Reflection.

-Emotional wellbeing affects physical wellbeing.

Event 38. The Clothes Peg.

-Physical world, mind and other dimensional activity all interact.

Event 39. Hinchinbrook Island.

-Dreams definitely can come true.

Event 40. Olive Oil!

-An invisible authoritarian voice offers good advice.

Event 41. Lavender Oil!

-Voices from another dimension.

Event 42. Mrs Priestly.

-Thoughts extend beyond our headspace into the cosmos.

-We are all interconnected in a bigger brain.

Event 43. Merrilly.

-Intercepting thoughts.

-Vibrational highways.

-Fine tuning for better reception and less interference.

Event 44. Mum Passes Over and Spends Time with Me.

-Only death of the physical body exists.

-Personality continues beyond physical death.

-Raising our sensitivity to the more that we are.

Printed in the United States
By Bookmasters